ANGOSTURA®
bitters cocktails

More Than 70 Classic
Recipes and Fancy Drinks

ANGOSTURA® bitters cocktails

More Than 70 Classic Recipes and Fancy Drinks

Countryman Press

An Imprint of W. W. Norton & Company
Independent Publishers Since 1923

CONTENTS

INTRODUCTION: 200 YEARS OF ANGOSTURA BITTERS
6

PART 1. COCKTAILS
25

THREE-INGREDIENT CLASSICS
27

DRINKS FOR SUNNY DAYS
51

SHAKEN NOT STIRRED
75

SPIRITED DRINKS
99

I'M NOT DRINKING, BUT MAKE IT DELICIOUS
123

APERITIFS
147

DIGESTIFS
171

PART 2. FOOD
195

SAVORY
196

SWEET
198

ACKNOWLEDGMENTS
200

INDEX
202

INTRODUCTION
200 YEARS OF ANGOSTURA BITTERS

While it's now known as an essential ingredient for any cocktail lover, the first batch of our bitters was made by a doctor to relieve his patients' digestive and stomach disorders. The special tonic was developed in 1824 by Dr. Johann Siegert, the surgeon general in Simón Bolívar's revolutionary army in Venezuela. Originally named Amargo Aromatico, or Aromatic Bitters it proved particularly popular with visiting sailors looking to quell their seasickness. It wasn't long before these sailors discovered that adding a dash or two of bitters to their ration of gin enhanced the flavor, creating one of the first Angostura cocktails—the Pink Gin—in the process.

In 1830, the tonic, now known as Dr. Siegert's aromatic bitters, was exported for the first time to Trinidad and to England. The bitters later became known as Angostura® aromatic bitters, taking its name from the town where it was created, Angostura in Venezuela, today known as Ciudad Bolívar. Dr. Siegert continued to practice medicine for another 20 years before resigning to devote his full attention to the commercial development of his bitters.

In 1875, Dr. Siegert's sons left Venezuela in possession of the secret formula for the bitters. They started production in Port of Spain, Trinidad, later setting up a rum distillery in Laventille in Trinidad and Tobago in 1949. The bitters have been produced here ever since and are made to exactly the same recipe Dr. Siegert created 200 years ago.

Even though it's made on a small island, Angostura bitters have been renowned across the world since their creation and picked up a number of prestigious awards in London, Paris, and Vienna in the 19th century. By the early 20th century, Angostura was appointed as purveyor to a number of royal households in Europe, including King Wilhelm II of Prussia, King Alfonso XIII of Spain, and King George V of Great Britain. In 1955, the company received a royal warrant from Queen Elizabeth II, who later visited the distillery in Trinidad and Tobago.

While there have been many twists and turns over the past 200 years, with the Trinidadian government even having to step in twice to keep production in Trinidad and Tobago, it was a golden age of cocktails that helped establish the bitters for centuries to come. One of the first recorded definitions of a cocktail, from a local paper in New York in 1806, calls it "a stimulating liquor, composed of spirits of any kind, sugar, water and bitters." Since then, bitters have become an essential ingredient in some of our favorite cocktails. Without them, the Old-Fashioned, Manhattan, and Champagne Cocktail simply would not exist today. In Harry Craddock's seminal work, *The Savoy Cocktail Book*, first published in 1930, more than 90 recipes mentioned Angostura bitters specifically by name.

Over the last 200 years, Angostura has never stopped innovating. From the creation of an award-winning rum portfolio, an amaro, and a line of bitters-based refreshers to the creation of orange bitters in 2007 and cocoa bitters in 2020, the company has always been on top of what's trending in the cocktail world. Its commitment to quality means Angostura bitters have stood the test of time and remain as revered today as when they were created 200 years ago.

A JEWEL OF TRINIDAD AND TOBAGO

Today, Angostura is one of Trinidad and Tobago's crown jewels, and its two centuries of history are a testament to the company's ambitious thinking and diverse cultural influences.

Trinidad and Tobago has the incredible white sandy beaches, crystal clear turquoise waters, and windswept palm trees we've come to expect from the Caribbean, as well as the most exquisite Hindu temples and a lively food and music scene. As a historically important commercial transit port, Trinidad has become an industrialized, metropolitan island, with a diverse mixture of cultures, which can be seen in everything from its distinctive food and drink to music and art.

Trinidad is blessed with an abundance of flora and fauna, including more than 100 species of butterflies and 18 species of hummingbirds. Incredible botanicals, bountiful ingredients, and an appreciation for diverse flavors influence the vibrant food and drink on the island.

Culturally, Trinidadians are very creative people. Everything on the island has a sense of theater, from swizzling a cocktail to dancing in the streets on Carnival Monday and Tuesday. Trinidad Carnival is world famous, and the energy that flows through the streets cannot be replicated anywhere else.

The techniques and knowledge of distilling in Trinidad came from the Portuguese Fernandes family. One of the first blenders and distillers on the islands, the Fernandes distillery was later acquired by and merged with Angostura. The style of rum produced by Angostura reflects the myriad influences from the British, Spanish, Portuguese, and French on Trinidad and Tobago.

There is a palpable pride from Trinidadians at the global success of Angostura. It really means something that they can find that distinctive oversized label and yellow cap behind just about any bar in the world and know it came from home.

ANGOSTURA® orange bitters
FROM THE HOUSE OF ANGOSTURA
Since 1824
ANGOSTURA
orange bitters
A SKILLFULLY BLENDED PREPARATION OF A VARIETY OF ORANGE EXTRACTS AND SPICES.
INGREDIENTS: WATER, GLYCERINE, ALCOHOL, NATURAL ORANGE SPICE FLAVOUR, NATURAL FLAVOURS, BETA-CAROTENE (COLOUR)
alc. 28.0% vol.
MANUFACTURED BY ANGOSTURA LTD. PORT OF SPAIN, TRINIDAD W.I.
100ml e
ANGOSTURA® cocoa bitters
THE HOUSE OF ANGOSTURA
Since 1824
ANGOSTURA
cocoa bitters
A DISTINCTIVE EXPRESSION EXPERTLY CRAFTED WITH FINE TRINITARIO COCOA NIBS
aromatic bitters
BY APPOINTMENT TO HER MAJESTY QUEEN ELIZABETH II MANUFACTURERS OF ANGOSTURA® aromatic bitters ANGOSTURA LIMITED
ANGOSTURA
aromatic bitters
44.7% alc./vol.
alc. 44.7% vol.
200 ml e
PRODUCT OF TRINIDAD & TOBAGO

A STORY IN EVERY DASH

THAT LABEL

With its oversized label and bright yellow cap, a bottle of Angostura bitters is instantly recognizable. But did you know that this iconic look was the product of a tight deadline? Two of the Siegert brothers were entering their father's recipe into a number of international competitions, and one was in charge of creating the bottle while the other worked on the label. When the two came together, they discovered that their creations didn't quite fit together. It's unknown whether the bottle was too small or the label was too big, but the brothers had run out of time, so the bottle was entered as it was.

While the creation of the oversized label was a happy accident, the decision to stick with it for all these years was a stroke of marketing genius.

THE SECRET TO SUCCESS

Angostura's success is in part due to its ability to keep a secret. The botanicals in the bitters are weighed out in a secret room within the distillery. Only five people are privy to that specific recipe, and none of them knows who the others are. Each of these manufacturers measures their individual portion inside that room, alone and away from prying eyes.

The Trinidadian government also assists in keeping the recipe secret. The botanicals are imported into Trinidad and Tobago using a coded number system. It's even written into law that no government official can ask for or disclose the contents of the botanicals being imported for the production of the bitters. It no longer takes a family, but a whole island, to keep Angostura's recipe a secret.

THE MEDALS

The medals that grace the label of every bottle of Angostura bitters depict both sides of the Medal of Excellence that Angostura was awarded at the Grand Exhibition in Vienna in 1873. These medals, combined with the signature of Dr. Siegert, make up the bitters' trademark and act as a warning to potential imitators.

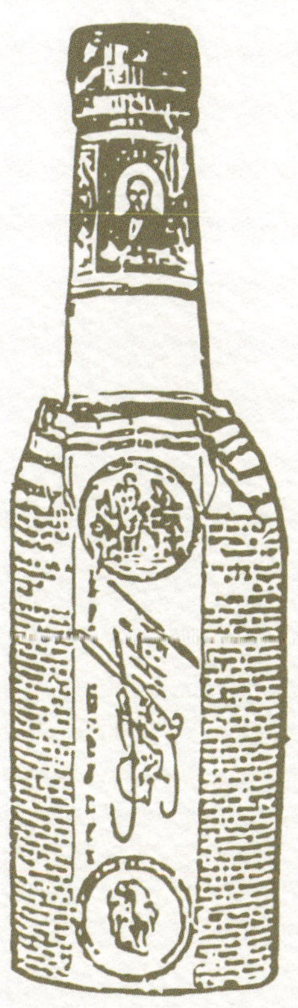

BY ROYAL APPOINTMENT

Angostura is the first and only Caribbean company to hold a royal warrant. In 1955, Queen Elizabeth II awarded Angostura bitters its royal warrant and, 30 years later, she visited the House of Angostura in Trinidad and Tobago.

SURPRISING ALTERNATIVE USES FOR BITTERS

Our bitters are known as both culinary and cocktail ingredients, but there are also some rather surprising additional uses for the bitters. Canon, a cocktail bar in Seattle, used copious amounts of bitters to stain its bar a deep mahogany color. In the Caribbean, rubbing bitters on your skin is said to make an excellent mosquito repellent. It will likely also stain your skin, so it's maybe not the best first option!

STYLES OF DRINKS

Bitters became synonymous with cocktails from the very beginning, helping to perfect flavorful drinks that stimulate the senses.

A great cocktail must be balanced and pleasing to the palate, nose, and eye. An outstanding cocktail is a full sensory experience. Balance in cocktails is all about proportions, finding the perfect place between tart and sweet, strong and weak, to create a drink that is more than the sum of its parts, in which no single element overshadows or outshines any other.

Bitters act as a pro tool to help bring drinks into balance. Our bitters can bind together ingredients and balance them, all while adding a rich, complex depth of flavor. There are a number of different cocktail styles outlined in this book, which have stood the test of time and spawned countless variations. Understanding the basic principles behind each style can help you be more creative in your cocktail experiments.

HIGHBALL

As well as being the name of a tall glass, a highball is a long, refreshing drink that includes a spirit and a carbonated mixer. Whisky and soda have become synonymous as the default choice for a highball and can be a delicious aperitif. Ice is the unspoken ingredient here—the more you have, the colder and more delicious the highball, so pack the glass full. The trick to a good highball is to not over-stir, lest you agitate the bubbles too much and lose the effervescence of the drink. Refrigerate your soda if you can before pouring, as colder soda retains more bubbles.

MARTINI

The martini is the original king of cocktails and is quite literally an icon. In the first edition of Harry Craddock's *The Savoy Cocktail Book*, a classic martini called for equal measures of gin, French vermouth, and a dash of orange bitters. Today, the Fifty-Fifty Martini is back in fashion in some quarters, but a dry martini will typically call for a ratio of between 3:1 and 5:1 gin to dry vermouth. The craft cocktail revival of the early 2000s saw the dry martini with orange bitters take center stage once more due to that zesty lift.

SOUR

A sour is a very old and broad category of cocktail that includes a spirit, citrus, and sweetener, often with bitters and egg white. The classic ratio for a sour is two parts spirit, one part citrus, and half a part sugar. A sour will always be shaken, never stirred, in order to fully integrate the citrus and egg white. Sours have that perfect balance of tart and sweet, and a beautiful velvety texture and mouthfeel.

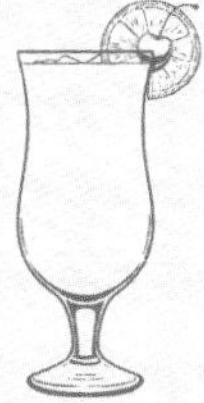

SWIZZLE

A swizzle is a style of drink defined less by its ingredients than the motion required to make it. Typically, this is a rum-based drink with citrus (usually lime), sweetener, and bitters. To make the drink, take a swizzle stick between the palms of both hands and rub them back and forth quickly. The swizzle stick was created from the branch of a tree native to the Caribbean with little prongs at the end that act as a whisk and churn up ice in crushed-ice drinks.

SLING

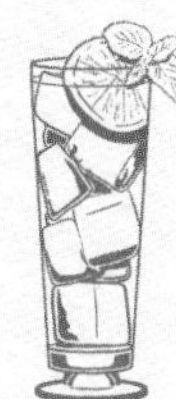

Slings first became popular toward the end of the 18th century, predating other types of cocktail. At its simplest, a sling is a mix of spirit, sugar, and water. The most famous is the Singapore Sling, which includes gin, citrus, liqueurs, and other sweeteners.

COCKTAIL KIT

There are a few key pieces of equipment you need to make drinks with bitters. While you can always get more fancy as you go, here are the basics to start mixing fancy drinks.

SHAKER

If you invest in one thing, a good shaker is an essential part of any kit. They're not superexpensive and will certainly help raise your cocktail game. A three-piece shaker is great for mixing individual drinks, and a two-piece Boston shaker can be easier when making multiple servings. Either works well.

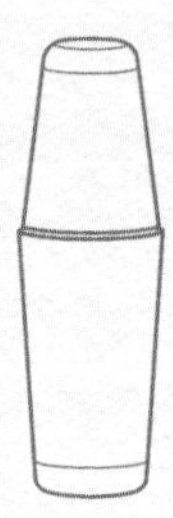

MIXING GLASS

Having a mixing glass on hand for stirred drinks such as martinis is ideal. But if you don't have one on hand, you can use the glass of a French press. If using an alternative, the glass may be a little thinner so take care. Or simply stir in one part of a cocktail shaker.

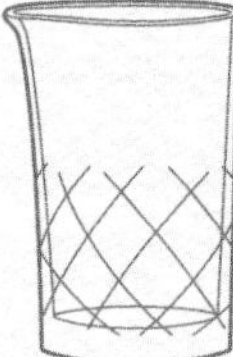

JIGGER

Getting the proportions right is the key to consistently good drinks, and measuring your spirits in a jigger is a pro move. Hourglass-shaped jiggers with two different measures on each end are widely available and aren't that expensive. However, if you don't have a jigger handy, you can use a shot glass or scaled measuring cups.

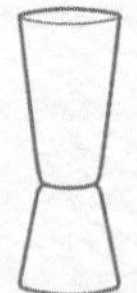

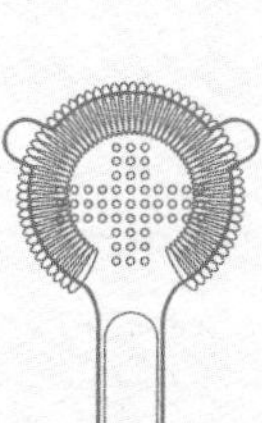

STRAINER
A strainer is the best way to ensure your drinks are both delicious to drink and pleasing to look at. A Hawthorne strainer will ensure solid ingredients such as fruit or herbs don't make their way into the drink, while a fine mesh strainer will stop even small shards of ice from passing through and is ideal when you want a crystal clear drink.

MUDDLER
A muddler is a sturdy tool to bruise and smash ingredients to release the juices and oils. If you don't have one on hand, use the end of a rolling pin or a wooden spoon.

SWIZZLE STICK
You can't make a swizzle without a swizzle stick, which comes from the branches of the swizzlestick tree (*Quararibea turbinata*), a species native to the Caribbean, where the tradition of swizzling stems from. This is one tool we recommend that you order, as it'll add some nice theater to your drink making and be a great talking point while you're entertaining.

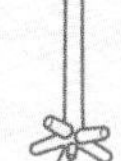

BARSPOON
A long, metal barspoon is necessary for stirring drinks to perfection. It can also double up as a measuring tool: A barspoon is equivalent to 1 teaspoon (5 ml).

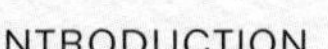

ANGOSTURA® orange bitters
FROM THE HOUSE OF ANGOSTURA
ANGOSTURA®
orange bitters
A SKILLFULLY BLENDED PREPARATION OF A VARIETY OF ORANGE EXTRACTS AND SPICES
INGREDIENTS: WATER, GLYCERINE, ALCOHOL, NATURAL ORANGE SPICE FLAVOUR, NATURAL FLAVOURS, BETA-CAROTENE (COLOUR)
alc. 28.0% vol.
100ml ℮

GLASSES

The choice of glassware adds to a drink and its visual appeal, so fancy glassware helps make fancy drinks. Most of the cocktails in this book can be made using just the first three styles of glass, but if you want to invest in more, here's a little overview.

HIGHBALL

A tall glass that's ideal for serving mixed drinks with plenty of ice.

ROCKS GLASS

This is a short, sturdy, wide-rimmed glass with a strong base that traditionally took a beating when sugar was being pummeled in it to make an Old-Fashioned.

COUPE

A coupe is a Champagne saucer with a long stem and shallow bowl and is a classic choice for fancy drinks served without ice. The coupe's wide rim makes for easy sipping with an elegant touch. You should hold the glass by the stem, not the bowl, even when serving, so as not to warm the icy cold drink inside.

MARTINI

This is a classic cocktail glass that's similar to a coupe, but usually it has straight angular sides.

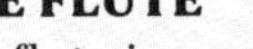

CHAMPAGNE FLUTE

A Champagne flute is another stemmed glass but with a tall slender shape and narrower rim to preserve more of the bubbles from Champagne. This glass helps to elevate any occasion and screams sophistication. A coupe can serve as a substitute for this glass as needed.

NICK & NORA

A stemmed glass with a higher-sided bowl, which means it can hold more liquid with less risk of spilling during bustling parties—a fact that has made it a favorite in bars and home bars alike. Save your carpets and get a few of these for dinner parties.

OTHER SPECIALITY GLASSES

There are many other speciality glasses that look superb and make a statement. A **hurricane glass** is curvaceous, with a flared rim that showcases the aromatics of tropical drinks wonderfully and leaves plenty of space for creative garnishes. The **pearl diver glass** is perfect for tropical drinks, while the bulbous **brandy snifter** was originally designed to capture the delicate aromatics of cognac but can work equally well for cocktails. A **cordial glass** is small and short-stemmed and is ideal for a neat aperitif.

THE ANGOSTURA BITTERS LINEUP

You are no doubt familiar with Angostura® aromatic bitters, which have been helping to make drinks more delicious for 200 years and are easily identifiable by that iconic oversized label and yellow cap.

But are you familiar with the rest of the Angostura range, developed with deep-rooted expertise in botanicals and bitters mixed with a little creative flair?

ANGOSTURA® AROMATIC BITTERS

Angostura aromatic bitters are the gold standard in bitters—their quality, consistency, and ability to bind, balance, enhance, and elevate drinks are unparalleled.

Bartenders all over the world use these bitters to elevate their cocktails—they work particularly well with aged spirits, such as whiskey, bourbon, rum, and pisco. As many drinks lovers will know, they're the essential ingredient in a Manhattan and an Old-Fashioned. They have often been called the salt and pepper of the bar world for their ability to enhance a drink and marry flavors together. While you may not notice the bitters in your drink, you'll surely notice their absence.

ANGOSTURA® ORANGE BITTERS

The award-winning orange bitters enliven cocktails with a deep citrus burst of brightness, which amplifies and infuses drinks with unrivaled layers of orange flavor and warming notes of aromatic spices to finish. They work well with white spirits, such as rum, gin, tequila, and vodka, where they brighten cocktails, elegantly accentuating the citrus tang in a Martini, Margarita, or Daiquiri.

The orange bitters are crafted by combining citrus essences from both sun-ripened bitter and lusciously sweet oranges, harmoniously balanced by a rich medley of herbs and spices.

ANGOSTURA® COCOA BITTERS

The cocoa bitters are a celebration of Angostura's provenance as they contain nibs of Trinidad and Tobago's agricultural gem, the indigenous Trinitario cocoa. Trinitario is one of the world's finest hybrid cocoas and was developed in Trinidad and Tobago more than 250 years ago. Trinitario is highly valued by chocolatiers all over the world for its distinctive bold, fruity, and often floral flavor. The bitters use the nibs to provide top notes of rich, floral, nutty cocoa, combining them with an intoxicating infusion of aromatic botanicals.

The cocoa bitters pair perfectly with sweet vermouth or aged spirits, such as whiskey, rum, cognac, and tequila. It works incredibly well in coffee drinks, such as the classic Espresso Martini (page 174) and the Café Trinidad (page 184).

ANGOSTURA®
200-YEAR ANNIVERSARY
LIMITED EDITION BITTERS

To mark its 200-year anniversary, Angostura unveiled a limited edition commemorative blend of bitters that pays tribute to two centuries of unparalleled craftsmanship and flavor mastery. These bitters stand out for their distinctive blend of premium botanicals, such as aged rum, angelica root, Roman wormwood, and nutmeg. Unlike standard bitters, they offer a luxurious flavor profile with nuanced notes of cardamom, orange, and earthy undertones, creating an elevated and unique taste experience.

A key botanical ingredient in many traditional bitters recipes, Roman wormwood adds complexity and depth to the blend, while angelica root provides herbal, earthy, and slightly sweet notes. With a limited batch of 120,000 bottles, why not use this unique ingredient in the following two celebratory cocktails and savor something truly special?

CLASSIQUE

Rich, elegant, opulent

This simple yet sophisticated cocktail celebrates four iconic leaders of their categories. The base of this drink is Angostura® 1824 rum, so named after the year the bitters were created. This elegant drink is elevated by Lillet Blanc aperitif wine, Champagne, and the very special limited-release Angostura® 200-year anniversary limited edition bitters.

INGREDIENTS

- 1¾ ounces Angostura® 1824 rum
- ¾ ounce Lillet Blanc aperitif wine
- 2 dashes Angostura® 200-year anniversary limited edition bitters
- 1 ounce Champagne

GARNISH

* Brandied cherry

GLASS

* Elegant coupe, chilled

METHOD

1. Add the rum, Lillet Blanc, and bitters to a mixing glass.
2. Add ice and stir for 15 seconds until well chilled.
3. Strain into a chilled coupe.
4. Top with the Champagne and garnish with a brandied cherry.

VIP PALOMA

Fresh, vibrant, fruity

The Paloma is the most popular tequila-based cocktail in Mexico; it's vibrantly refreshing and simultaneously sweet, sour, and bitter. This VIP Paloma is elevated by the addition of Angostura® 200-year anniversary limited edition bitters and prosecco. It's a bubbly beauty of a drink.

INGREDIENTS

- 1½ ounces 100% agave reposado tequila
- 3 ounces grapefruit soda
- 2 dashes Angostura® 200-year anniversary limited edition bitters
- Prosecco to top

GARNISH

* Grapefruit wedge and fresh rosemary sprig

GLASS

* Highball

METHOD

1. Add the tequila to a highball glass filled with ice.
2. Add the grapefruit soda and bitters and stir gently.
3. Top with prosecco.
4. Garnish with a grapefruit wedge and a sprig of rosemary.

In the modern age, mixology has surpassed its traditional boundaries and made its mark in unexpected places. Whether you're concocting a quick mixer for a cozy date night, crafting an impressive libation to dazzle friends, or even opting for a sophisticated creation sans liquor, the concept of a "cocktail" has evolved to take on various definitions.

Although it may appear complex, the world of mixology offers a rich canvas of recipes to inspire your inner bartender. From seasoned mixologists to eager beginners, this collection of recipes encourages everyone to explore and experiment. Each recipe celebrates the artistry and versatility of classic cocktails, inviting you to craft drinks for any occasion with a flair and finesse that are uniquely yours.

PART 1. COCKTAILS

★

ANGOSTURA® aromatic bitters
THE HOUSE OF ANGOSTURA
BY APPOINTMENT TO HER
MAJESTY QUEEN ELIZABETH II
MANUFACTURERS OF
ANGOSTURA® aromatic bitters
ANGOSTURA LIMITED
ANGOSTURA
aromatic bitters
44.7% alc./vol.
alc. 44.7% vol.
200 ml℮
PRODUCT OF TRINIDAD & TOBAGO

THREE-INGREDIENT CLASSICS

Three is the magic number. This chapter proves drinks don't need to be complicated to be delicious. When there are fewer ingredients, the proportions and careful balance of how the drink is put together become even more important.

You'll find two of the three best-loved classic cocktails in this chapter: the Old-Fashioned and the Manhattan.

A STORY IN EVERY DASH: THE OLD-FASHIONED

Evolved from the Whiskey Cocktail, the Old-Fashioned was first referenced in 1888 in *The Bartender's Manual* by Theodore Proulx and predates both the Martini and the Manhattan.

It's one of only a few drinks that spawned the name of a glass used to make it, being built in a heavy-bottomed squat glass often referred to as an old-fashioned glass. According to the original recipe, a sugar cube soaked in bitters was muddled into a paste with a barspoon of warm water before whiskey and ice were added, which meant the glass would need to be pretty thick and sturdy to withstand regular bashing.

Nowadays, simple syrup is often used in place of a sugar cube to somewhat speed up the creation of this drink, but it still takes a little time to make, which is rewarded by the liquid in the glass.

The Old-Fashioned survived Prohibition in the United States, which outlawed the production of its core ingredient, whiskey, and came back stronger for it. By the 1940s and 1950s, it was almost an essential on every bar menu. Today, the Old-Fashioned is still very much in fashion.

OLD-FASHIONED

Sweet, rich, spirit-forward

Beloved by whiskey fans the world over, the original whiskey cocktail has taken many forms and at one point veered into a fruity drink served long over ice. That's when drinkers started to call for the "old-fashioned" whiskey cocktail they knew and loved. More than a century later, the name has stuck. It's the very definition of a cocktail—spirits, water, sugar, and bitters—and is considered a national institution by many in the United States.

INGREDIENTS

- 2 ounces bourbon or rye whiskey
- 1 teaspoon simple syrup
- 2 dashes Angostura® aromatic bitters

GARNISH

* Orange twist

GLASS

* Rocks

METHOD

1. Pour half of the whiskey into a rocks glass, add a couple of ice cubes, and stir.
2. Add the simple syrup, bitters, and a couple more ice cubes and stir some more.
3. Add the remaining whiskey and some more ice and, guess what, stir again.
4. Garnish with an orange twist.

Some say rye whiskey is the traditional spirit here, and using rye means the drink packs more of a punch and has a delicious, spicy kick. Others favor bourbon, which leads to a mellower, softer Old-Fashioned.

STONE FENCE

Sweet, tart, spicy

This simplest of American highballs dates back to the Colonial era and was originally made with rum as the base. By 1862, Jerry Thomas's *Bar-Tender's Guide* called for this drink with bourbon; after Prohibition, Scotch became a popular base. It's a wonderfully flavorful autumnal drink that works with whatever dark spirit you happen to have.

INGREDIENTS

- 2 ounces aged rum, brandy, bourbon, or rye whiskey
- 1 dash Angostura® aromatic bitters
- 150ml fresh apple juice

GARNISH

* Fresh mint sprig, lemon twist, or freshly grated nutmeg

GLASS

* Highball

METHOD

1. Fill a highball glass with ice.
2. Add all the ingredients.
3. Stir gently.
4. Garnish with a mint sprig, lemon twist, or freshly grated nutmeg.

This is a versatile drink that you can adapt to whatever dark spirit you have on hand. Opting for bourbon brings notes of vanilla and caramel, rye brings on a nice baking spice, rum provides a rich sweetness, and brandy brings additional fruity, oaky notes.

THE CHAMPAGNE COCKTAIL

Opulent, aromatic, sparkling

This is one of the simplest and classiest cocktails that appeared in the original *Bar-Tender's Guide* in 1862. The base of this drink is a sugar cube soaked in bitters, which is then topped with Champagne. This drink is a treat for the senses. The Champagne slowly eats away at the sugar at the bottom, launching a persistent stream of fine bubbles while you sip.

INGREDIENTS

- 1 sugar cube
- 4 dashes Angostura® aromatic bitters
- Champagne to top

GARNISH

* Lemon twist or a brandied cherry

GLASS

* Champagne flute

METHOD

1. Place the sugar cube at the bottom of a flute.
2. Add the bitters until the sugar cube is soaked.
3. Fill the glass with Champagne and garnish with a lemon twist or brandied cherry.

Add ⅓ ounce of cognac on top of the bitters-soaked sugar cube for an extra layer of flavor and complexity.

JAPANESE COCKTAIL

Rich, sweet, nutty

A drink created by celebrated bartender "Professor" Jerry Thomas in the mid-19th century, the Japanese Cocktail is thought to pay homage to one of Thomas's patrons, Tateishi Onojirō-Noriyuki. He was an interpreter on Japan's first diplomatic mission to America in 1860 and seemed to have a ball at Thomas's bar. The rich fruity elegance of the cognac combined with the sweet nuttiness of orgeat is balanced by a couple of dashes of bitters.

INGREDIENTS

- 2 ounces cognac
- ⅓ ounce orgeat syrup
- 2 dashes Angostura® aromatic bitters

GARNISH

* Lemon twist

GLASS

* Coupe, chilled

METHOD

1. Add all the ingredients to a cocktail shaker.
2. Add ice and shake for 30 seconds until well chilled.
3. Strain into a chilled coupe and garnish with a lemon twist.

Orgeat, pronounced OR-zhaat, *is an almond syrup that adds a distinctive sweetness to drinks. It is a good amount of work to make but thankfully very easy to buy these days. It's also a key sweetener in many tropical drinks, so it's worth having in a home bar.*

MANHATTAN

Elegant, bittersweet, spicy

The origins of the Manhattan may be disputed, but unlike the Martini, most agree on the classic proportions: two parts whiskey to one part sweet vermouth, and a few dashes of bitters to balance and bind. This classic cocktail, first published in 1882, has never gone out of style. It's a combo that has become iconic and arguably one of the most riffed-upon drinks.

INGREDIENTS

- 2 ounces rye whiskey
- 1 ounce sweet vermouth
- 2 dashes Angostura® aromatic bitters

GARNISH

* Brandied cherry

GLASS

* Martini, chilled

METHOD

1. Combine all the ingredients in a mixing glass.
2. Half-fill with ice and stir for 20 seconds until well chilled.
3. Strain into a chilled martini glass.
4. Garnish with a brandied cherry.

If you prefer Scotch, switch out the rye for a single malt or blended Scotch, and you have a Rob Roy.

STAR

Rounded, sweet, elegant

A twist on a Manhattan that uses apple brandy instead of whiskey, the Star first found fame in the 1890s. Often made "perfect" with equal parts apple brandy and sweet vermouth with a couple of dashes of bitters, our version uses a 2:1 ratio of apple brandy to sweet vermouth. The use of apple brandy in place of rye makes this an elegantly fruity, more approachable type of Manhattan.

INGREDIENTS

- 2 ounces apple brandy
- 1 ounce sweet vermouth
- 2 dashes Angostura® aromatic bitters

GARNISH

* Brandied cherry

GLASS

* Coupe, chilled

METHOD

1. Add all the ingredients to a mixing glass.
2. Half-fill with ice and stir for 15–20 seconds until well chilled.
3. Strain into a chilled coupe.
4. Garnish with a brandied cherry.

We've dialed back the sweet vermouth here to adapt the original recipe for a modern palate, but play around with the proportions to suit your tastes.

TUXEDO

Savory, tangy, pungent

The Tuxedo cocktail dates back to the 1890s and takes its name not from the semiformal suit but from a private country club called the Tuxedo Club. Fino sherry is bone-dry and adds a nutty richness that is lifted by the citrus burst of orange bitters. At home at a black-tie dinner, this stylish, savory riff on a Martini has appeared in many esteemed cocktail books.

INGREDIENTS

- 2 ounces gin
- 1 ounce fino sherry
- 2 dashes Angostura® orange bitters

GARNISH

* Orange twist

GLASS

* Martini, chilled

METHOD

1. Add all the ingredients to a mixing glass.
2. Half-fill with ice and stir for 15–20 seconds until well chilled.
3. Strain into a chilled martini glass.
4. Garnish with an orange twist.

Like most Martini riffs, there are many variations on a Tuxedo. Some recipes call for a dash or two of maraschino liqueur to add sweetness or absinthe for a herbal note. You can also play with the ratio of gin to sherry, or opt for a richer style of sherry, such as an amontillado if you find fino too dry.

ALASKA

Sweet, herbaceous, spirited

This variation on a Martini, which confusingly is not from Alaska, uses yellow Chartreuse in place of vermouth for a hint of sweet herbs. Originally made with a sweet Old Tom gin, it's now made with a classic London dry gin, which is more readily available. This drink has enjoyed a cult following among cocktail enthusiasts since the early 1900s, as it provides a subtly sweet, herbaceous twist on a Martini.

INGREDIENTS

- 2 ounces gin
- ½ ounce yellow Chartreuse
- 3 dashes Angostura® orange bitters

GARNISH

* Lemon twist

GLASS

* Coupe, chilled

METHOD

1. Add all the ingredients to a mixing glass.
2. Half-fill with ice and stir for 30 seconds until well chilled.
3. Strain into a chilled coupe and garnish with a lemon twist.

As with a classic Martini, people's personal preferences with ratios vary wildly. If you like your drink a little sweeter, go harder on the yellow Chartreuse. If you want to retain just a hint of that herbal sweetness, play with a 5:1 or 6:1 ratio of gin to yellow Chartreuse.

RUM MANHATTAN

Rich, sweet, spicy

During Prohibition, it was much easier to get your hands on rum than rye whiskey, which had all but ceased production. The Rum Manhattan came into its own at this time as a twist on the classic cocktail that used rum in place of rye for a sweeter, rounder finish. The elegance of a Manhattan with the layered complexity and rich sweetness of a rum, combined with sweet vermouth and bitters, makes this a classic.

SINGREDIENTS

- 1⅓ ounces Angostura® 1824 rum
- ⅔ ounce sweet vermouth
- 1 dash Angostura® aromatic bitters

GARNISH

* Brandied cherry

GLASS

* Coupe, chilled

METHOD

1. Combine the rum, vermouth, and bitters in a mixing glass.
2. Half-fill with ice and stir for 30 seconds until well chilled.
3. Strain into a chilled coupe and garnish with a brandied cherry.

This is a recipe where the rum is allowed to shine and be the star of the show, so use a good-quality aged rum and let the bitters bind the flavors together.

THE BENNETT

Tangy, citrusy, spicy

The Bennett was featured in the 1922 cocktail book, *Cocktails: How to Mix Them*, and was originally made with Old Tom gin, lime, and a few good dashes of bitters. Modern iterations popularized by Meaghan Dorman at The Bennett in New York call for the more popular London dry gin. It's a refreshing gimlet, and with a couple of dashes of bitters, what's not to love?

INGREDIENTS

- 2 ounces gin
- 1 ounce fresh lime juice
- ½ ounce simple syrup
- 2 dashes Angostura® aromatic bitters

GARNISH

* Lime wheel

GLASS

* Martini, chilled

METHOD

1. Add all the ingredients to a cocktail shaker.
2. Half-fill with ice and shake for 20 seconds until well chilled.
3. Strain into a chilled martini glass and garnish with a lime wheel.

If you're being fancy, you can replace the lime juice and simple syrup with an elevated lime cordial. Take equal parts sugar and lime juice and infuse with fresh lime zest and cinnamon spice. Strain and bottle.

ANGOSTURA aromatic bitters
BY APPOINTMENT TO HER MAJESTY QUEEN ELIZABETH II MANUFACTURERS OF ANGOSTURA® aromatic bitters ANGOSTURA LIMITED
ANGOSTURA
aromatic bitters
44.7% alc./vol.
alc. 44.7% vol.
200 ml℮
PRODUCT OF TRINIDAD & TOBAGO

★

DRINKS FOR SUNNY DAYS

Is there any better way to cool off on a hot, sunny day than with a crisp cocktail? This is a collection of classic cocktails and modern drinks that sings of sunshine.

While these sunny-day cocktails are great fun, they can also be serious and sophisticated drinks. The classic combination of rum, sugar, lime, and bitters in a Daiquiri can be every bit as elegant as a Martini or a Manhattan. Beyond rum, there's a great whiskey twist on a Mai Tai with the Rye Tai, a tropical tequila drink with Doctor Limebender, and a gin homage to summer and Snoop Dogg's classic "Gin and Juice."

A STORY IN EVERY DASH: THE QUEEN'S PARK SWIZZLE

The Queen's Park Swizzle was the signature cocktail at the Queen's Park Hotel, a luxury tropical getaway in Trinidad and Tobago. In its 1920s heyday, it served sophisticated drinks to thirsty, well-heeled travelers.

A rum-based drink served over crushed ice, the Queen's Park Swizzle is a refreshing blend of sour and sweet. Pungent mint and freshly squeezed lime juice are balanced by demerara sugar and a generous quantity of bitters.

A swizzle is a style of drink that gets its name not from the ingredients or flavors but from the motion used to make it: swizzling. To make one, you need a swizzle stick, traditionally made from branches of the *Quararibea turbinata*, known as the swizzlestick tree. The branches of the tree, native to the Caribbean, end in little fingers that act like a whisk, which help to churn crushed ice in a theatrical fashion.

QUEEN'S PARK SWIZZLE

Colorful, vibrant, refreshing

Making this classic swizzle from Trinidad and Tobago is a spectacle and piece of theater in itself. It was created at the Queen's Park Hotel, an upscale 1920s tropical retreat in the beating heart of Port of Spain. It's a drink with color, vibrancy, and a ton of flavor, encapsulating Trinidad perfectly. The crucial ingredient is, of course, Trinidad and Tobago's very own bitters.

INGREDIENTS

- 12–14 fresh mint leaves
- 1 ounce fresh lime juice
- 1 ounce demerara simple syrup
- 2 ounces Angostura® 7-year-old rum
- 6–8 dashes Angostura® aromatic bitters

GARNISH

* Fresh mint sprig

GLASS

* Highball

METHOD

1. In a highball glass, muddle the mint leaves in the lime juice and simple syrup.
2. Fill the glass three-quarters full with dry crushed ice.
3. Pour the rum over the crushed ice and swizzle well (see below) until the glass is ice-cold and frosted.
4. Pack the glass with more crushed mint.

It isn't a swizzle unless it is swizzled. To execute this West Indian cocktail technique, simply put the swizzle stick in the drink, place it between your palms, and move them back and forth as quickly as you can.

SINGAPORE SLING

Tropical, lively, refreshing

The Singapore Sling is said to have been created at the Raffles Bar by a bartender named Ngiam Tong Boon. The cocktail at Raffles today is likely a lot sweeter and fruitier than the original recipe, which was said to be stronger with more herbal, citrus, and spice notes. This twist on a Gin Sling was created around the turn of the 20th century, and by the mid-1920s, the drink was known around the world.

INGREDIENTS

- 1½ ounces gin
- 1½ ounces fresh pineapple juice
- ½ ounce Bénédictine liqueur
- ¼ ounce Heering cherry liqueur
- ½ ounce fresh lime juice
- ¼ ounce orange liqueur
- 1 dash Angostura® aromatic bitters
- Chilled club soda to top

GARNISH

* Orange or pineapple slice and brandied cherry

GLASS

* Hurricane

METHOD

1. Add all the ingredients, except the club soda, into a shaker.
2. Add ice and shake for 10–15 seconds until well chilled and frothy.
3. Strain into a hurricane glass over fresh ice.
4. Top with chilled club soda.
5. Garnish with an orange or pineapple slice and a brandied cherry.

It's been said that no two Singapore Sling recipes are quite alike. So why not play around with the proportions as you prefer? We've held back on the pineapple here and ensured a good measure of gin for a Singapore Sling that is balanced and layered with a fruity, herbaceous bite.

DAIQUIRI

Refreshingly zesty, tangy

This classic combination of rum, sugar, lime, and bitters can be just as elegant as a Martini or Manhattan. Named after the harbor town of Daiquirí on Cuba's southern coast, this drink was perfected by a couple of Havana bars during Prohibition. Bar La Florida was known as the Cathedral of the Daiquiri in the 1920s, and it wasn't long before this drink was captivating revelers in US speakeasies.

INGREDIENTS

- 2 ounces Angostura® 1919 rum
- ¾ ounce fresh lime juice
- ½ ounce simple syrup
- 3 dashes Angostura® aromatic bitters

GARNISH

* Lime twist

GLASS

* Coupe, chilled

METHOD

1. Combine all the ingredients in a cocktail shaker.
2. Half-fill with ice and shake for 15 seconds until well chilled.
3. Strain into a chilled coupe and garnish with a lime twist.

Skip a Strawberry Daiquiri, which can overpower the rum, and opt instead for a version named after writer Ernest Hemingway. This twist uses ½ ounce of white grapefruit juice, a dash of maraschino cherry liqueur, and the rest of the classic Daiquiri ingredients, apart from the syrup. The result is a supertart, clean cocktail that is endlessly refreshing.

MAI TAI

Rich, zesty, sweet, nutty

This iconic drink came to define the tiki movement. The name is inspired by the Tahitian exclamation "Mai tai roa ae!", which means "Out of this world good!" Even though the original recipe was closely guarded by its creator, "Trader Vic" Victor Bergeron Jr., so many rum lovers asked for this drink in other bars that mixologists were forced to figure out their own interpretations to meet consumer demand.

INGREDIENTS

- 1 ounce Angostura® 5-year-old gold rum
- 1 ounce Angostura® reserva white rum
- 1 ounce orange curaçao
- ½ ounce fresh lime juice
- 1 teaspoon orgeat syrup
- ½ teaspoon granulated sugar
- 2 dashes Angostura® aromatic bitters

GARNISH

* Fresh mint sprig and lime wedge

GLASS

* Rocks

METHOD

1. Add all the ingredients to a cocktail shaker.
2. Half-fill with ice and shake for 15 seconds until well chilled.
3. Strain into an ice-filled rocks glass.
4. Garnish with a mint sprig and lime wedge.

The balance of sweet, sour, and bitterness means the Mai Tai works really well with food. Try it with island-inspired spiced marinated meats or zesty fresh seafood dishes.

OLD CUBAN

Decadent, crisp, lively

The Old Cuban is an elegant twist on a Mojito using a Champagne top and calling for an aged rum, hence the "old." Created in 2001 by the legendary Audrey Saunders, it provided a glamorous signature to the landmark Bemelmans Bar at the Carlyle Hotel in New York City. After it debuted at the Ritz in London, the Old Cuban was celebrated in the international press and started appearing on cocktail bar menus on both sides of the pond.

INGREDIENTS

- 6 fresh mint leaves
- ⅔ ounce fresh lime juice
- 1 ounce simple syrup
- 1½ ounces Angostura® 1919 rum
- 2 dashes Angostura® aromatic bitters
- 2 ounces Champagne

GARNISH

* Fresh mint sprig

GLASS

* Coupe

METHOD

1. Muddle the mint leaves with the lime juice and simple syrup in a cocktail shaker.
2. Add the rum, bitters, and some ice and shake well for 15 seconds until frothy.
3. Strain into a coupe and top with Champagne.
4. Garnish with a mint sprig.

FIVE ISLAND FIZZ

Citrusy, gentle heat, fizzy

The Five Island Fizz uses ingredients from five Caribbean islands: rum and bitters from Trinidad and Tobago, ginger beer from Barbuda, Jamaican limes, and Velvet Falernum, a distinctive liqueur from Barbados. All ingredients are easily combined in the glass to provide a thirst-quenching, tangy drink with a warming sweet spice. A twist on a mule, the ginger beer provides refreshing bubbles with a little prickle of heat and spice that builds with each sip.

David Delaney, US, Angostura Global Cocktail Challenge winner, 2012

INGREDIENTS

- 1½ ounces Angostura® 5-year-old rum
- ⅔ ounce Velvet Falernum
- ½ ounce fresh lime juice
- 2 dashes Angostura® aromatic bitters
- 1½ ounces Barritt's ginger beer
- ⅓ ounce liqueur from Luxardo maraschino cherries

GARNISH

* Lime wheel and brandied cherry

GLASS

* Highball

METHOD

1. Combine the rum, Velvet Falernum, lime juice, and bitters in a highball glass.
2. Fill with crushed ice.
3. Top with the ginger beer.
4. Add the liqueur from the cherries to provide the red top.
5. Garnish with a lime wheel wrapped around a brandied cherry.

Velvet Falernum is a Bajan classic liqueur used as a cocktail ingredient and is made with lime, almond, ginger, vanilla, and clove. It can be a pain to make but is easily available to buy.

RYE TAI

Tropical, soft, nutty, sweet

The Rye Tai packs a punch and is rounded out by pineapple juice for a refreshing drink that whiskey lovers can enjoy on long summer days. Here, the nutty orgeat is balanced by tart lemon, and the bitters top dances through the drink as you sip for a fun bit of visual theater. It's a simple, fruity, whiskey-based tropical cocktail made with rye for an extra bite. If it's not yet a modern classic, it should be!

INGREDIENTS

- 2 ounces rye whiskey
- ¾ ounce fresh pineapple juice
- ¾ ounce fresh lemon juice
- ¾ ounce orgeat syrup
- 6–10 dashes Angostura® aromatic bitters

GARNISH

* Pineapple wedge

GLASS

* Highball

METHOD

1. Combine the whiskey, pineapple and lemon juices, and orgeat in a cocktail shaker.
2. Half-fill with ice and shake for 30 seconds until well chilled.
3. Strain into a highball glass with crushed ice.
4. Top with the bitters and garnish with a pineapple wedge.

Pronounced OR-zhaat, *this almond syrup is a pain to make, so just buy it—it's an essential part of tropical drinks that can't be substituted.*

DOCTOR LIMEBENDER

Hot, spicy, fragrant

There's a tiki tradition of naming drinks after doctors, and this is our twist on the Doctor Mindbender, a devilishly good cocktail created by Death & Co's Matthew Belanger. It has the intense floral flavor of habanero chilies and the fruity sweetness of guava syrup in place of grenadine. It's a riff on a Mexican Firing Squad—a tart, refreshing classic—but our version turns up the heat with habanero-infused tequila.

INGREDIENTS

- 1¾ ounces habanero-infused tequila (see below)
- ⅔ ounce guava syrup
- ⅔ ounce fresh lime juice
- 2 dashes Angostura® aromatic bitters

GARNISH

* Lime wheel

GLASS

* Hurricane

METHOD

1. Add all the ingredients to a cocktail shaker.
2. Half-fill with ice and short shake for 10–15 seconds.
3. Strain into a hurricane glass filled with cracked ice.
4. Garnish with a lime wheel.

To make habanero-infused tequila, take 3 habanero chili peppers, remove the stems and seeds, and cut into strips. Add to a bottle of your favorite blanco 100% agave tequila. Leave it to rest at room temperature overnight and strain through a cheesecloth or sieve. Store in a cool dry place.

BUTTERFLY SWIZZLE

Tropical, tangy, aromatic

The swizzle is both a technique and a style of drink. To swizzle is a theatrical Caribbean bartending technique that uses a swizzle stick to mix a crushed ice drink. This is a swizzle inspired by the butterflies that went into the sugarcane fields as a sign that the sugarcane was ready to harvest. A swizzle is always a fancy drink, as it's made with such flair and theater.

Mike Jordhoy, France, Angostura Global Cocktail Challenge finalist, 2020

INGREDIENTS

- 1⅓ ounces Angostura® 7-year-old rum
- ½ ounce banana liqueur
- ⅓ ounce fresh lime juice
- ⅓ ounce simple syrup
- 1 teaspoon amaro di Angostura®
- 4 dashes absinthe
- 2 dashes Angostura® orange bitters
- 5 dashes Angostura® aromatic bitters

GARNISH

* Flamed banana wedge (see below)

GLASS

* Snifter

METHOD

1. Build the drink in a snifter, except the bitters.
2. Add some dry crushed ice and swizzle.
3. Finish with more ice and the bitters.
4. Garnish with a flamed banana wedge.

To flame a banana, preheat a heavy-bottomed pan over medium-high heat, toss in some butter, add some sugar, and stir until dissolved. Add banana slices, then stir and flip until evenly coated, and sizzle for 3–4 minutes. Carefully tilt the pan away from you and away from the heat and add a splash of rum. Jiggle the pan a little until the rum ignites. Once the flames die down, swirl the sauce in the pan a little more. If using an electric stove, hold a lighter near the pan to ignite.

SIPPIN' ON GIN AND JUICE

Tropical, tangy, fragrant

Named after the iconic 1994 Snoop Dogg track, "Gin and Juice," this pretty summer sipper is giving laid-back sunny days. A chilled mix of hibiscus-and-rosehip-infused gin combined with a splash of pineapple, lime, orgeat, triple sec, and bitters for the win. Did you know it was Snoop's mom who first introduced him to the joys of gin and juice?

Don Ranasinghe, Smoke & Bitters, Sri Lanka

INGREDIENTS

- 2 ounces hibiscus-and-rosehip-infused gin (see below)
- ½ ounce orgeat syrup
- ½ ounce triple sec
- 1¼ ounces fresh pineapple juice
- ⅔ ounce fresh lime juice
- 2 dashes Angostura® aromatic bitters

GARNISH

* Orange wheel, fresh cranberries, and fresh rosemary sprig

GLASS

* Rocks

METHOD

1. Combine all the ingredients in a cocktail shaker.
2. Add ice and shake for 15 seconds until well chilled.
3. Strain into a rocks glass with one big ice cube.
4. Garnish with an orange wheel, cranberries, and rosemary sprig.

To infuse gin with hibiscus and rose, place 1 ounce dried hibiscus and 1 ounce dried rose hips in a 750-milliliter bottle of gin and cold-infuse in the fridge for 24 hours. Strain through a coffee filter.

BY APPOINTMENT TO HER MAJESTY QUEEN ELIZABETH II MANUFACTURERS OF ANGOSTURA® aromatic bitters ANGOSTURA LIMITED
ANGOSTURA
aromatic bitters
44.7% alc./vol.
alc. 44.7% vol
200 mle
PRODUCT OF TRINIDAD & TOBAGO

★

SHAKEN NOT STIRRED

The rhythmic sound of a cocktail being shaken is the perfect way to build anticipation for the drink that follows. It's a great piece of theater, but what is all that shaking actually doing? It not only chills the drink and combines ingredients but also provides aeration and texture to the liquid.

Many drinks using fruit juices or egg whites need to be shaken for the ingredients to be properly combined. Included are two sours—a New York Sour with an attractive red top and a Pisco Sour with pretty swirls of bitters on its frothy foam—as well as classics, such as the Margarita, and underground favorites that have become modern classics, including the London Calling.

A STORY IN EVERY DASH: THE TRINIDAD SOUR

The Trinidad Sour is an unorthodox cocktail that upends convention by using bitters not to accentuate flavor, but as the base of the drink itself. On paper, it doesn't look like it'll work, and that is precisely why the drink has garnered such popularity—people, particularly bartenders, were curious as to what this cocktail would taste like.

Giuseppe González created the Trinidad Sour, inspired by a drink made by fellow Italian Valentino Bolognese, the Trinidad Especial. After González tested his recipe on his bartender friends, the drink ended up being served as a bartender's special in Boston, San Francisco, and London.

It's a cocktail that can be easily replicated with ingredients you'll find in any good cocktail bar—a hallmark of any modern classic. Ultimately, the cocktail's success is based on its unusual nature and memorability. The Trinidad Sour upsets the usual order of things, which makes it difficult to forget.

TRINIDAD SOUR

Earthy, velvety, aromatic

Giuseppe González created this modern classic in 2009 while at the Clover Club in New York City. Unusually, it uses bitters as the base "spirit," which made it a standout cocktail that was soon replicated across the world. It's now classified as an official cocktail by the International Bartenders Association, and all professional bartenders are expected to know how to make it.

INGREDIENTS

- 1½ ounces Angostura® aromatic bitters
- 1 ounce orgeat syrup
- ¾ ounce fresh lemon juice
- ½ ounce rye whiskey

GLASS

* Coupe, chilled

METHOD

1. Combine all the ingredients in a cocktail shaker.
2. Half-fill with ice and shake for 15 seconds until well chilled.
3. Strain into a chilled coupe.

Some bartenders choose to use egg white, a traditional sour ingredient, to give even more texture to this delicious drink.

NEW YORK SOUR

Silky, citrusy, sour

Strangely enough, the New York Sour was not created in New York State, but was likely later adopted and popularized by a bartender in the city. What makes a New York Sour unique is the distinctive red wine float. Egg white is also often added to the original recipe, which gives it a lovely velvety mouthfeel.

INGREDIENTS

- 2 ounces bourbon
- 1 ounce fresh lemon juice
- ½ ounce simple syrup
- 1 egg white
- 3 dashes Angostura® aromatic bitters
- ½ ounce red wine

GARNISH

* Lemon twist

GLASS

* Rocks

METHOD

1. Add all the ingredients, except the red wine, to a cocktail shaker without ice and dry-shake hard to whip up a foam.
2. Fill the shaker with ice and shake for 20 seconds until well chilled.
3. Fine strain into a rocks glass.
4. Fill the glass with ice, then top with a red wine float (see below).
5. Garnish with a lemon twist.

To help the red wine float, slowly pour it over the back of a spoon onto the surface of the drink, just under the frothy egg white, creating the signature attractive red top.

CLOVER CLUB

Zingy, bright, velvety

The Clover Club was named after a men's club in Philadelphia frequented by prominent reporters, which is possibly why this recipe was published as early as 1908. While it doesn't traditionally call for bitters, we think they add a certain something to this drink. This sweet, tart pre-Prohibition drink was revived by Julie Reiner when she opened a bar bearing its name in Brooklyn in 2008.

INGREDIENTS

- 2 ounces London dry gin
- 1 ounce French dry vermouth
- 1 teaspoon raspberry syrup
- 1 egg white
- ½ ounce simple syrup
- ½ teaspoon fresh lemon juice
- 3 dashes Angostura® aromatic bitters

GARNISH

* Fresh raspberries

GLASS

* Wine

METHOD

1. Combine all the ingredients, except the bitters, in a cocktail shaker.
2. Half-fill with ice and shake vigorously for 20 seconds until well chilled.
3. Strain into a small wine glass.
4. Add the bitters on top.
5. Garnish with fresh raspberries.

If you don't have raspberry syrup, muddle a few raspberries at the bottom of the shaker, add a little extra-rich simple syrup (2:1 sugar to water), and double strain.

PISCO SOUR

Light, zesty, aromatic

Pisco is an unoaked grape brandy that makes for a delicious sour. The Pisco Sour was created by Victor Vaughen Morris, an American expat who went to Peru to work on the railroads and missed his whiskey sour. Today, a Pisco Sour is known for its zingy combination of pisco and lime shaken with egg white. The Pisco Sour is a classic cocktail from the 1920s and Peru's national drink. The Peruvian government celebrates the drink as a distinctive part of Peru's culture and heritage.

INGREDIENTS

- 2 ounces pisco
- ¾ ounce simple syrup
- ⅔ ounce fresh lime juice
- 1 egg white
- 8–10 dashes Angostura® aromatic bitters

GLASS

* Coupe, chilled

METHOD

1. Add all the ingredients, except the bitters, to a cocktail shaker without ice.
2. Shake for 20 seconds until all the ingredients are well mixed.
3. Add some ice and shake for an additional 15 seconds until well chilled.
4. Strain into a chilled coupe.
5. Garnish with the bitters.

Add the bitters to the foam top and use a cocktail skewer to swirl it together to make pretty shapes.

THE LINE COCKTAIL

Rich, tangy, sweet

One of the earliest known classics to come from Japan, The Line Cocktail combines equal parts gin, Bénédictine, and sweet vermouth with a few dashes of bitters. Curiously for an all-spirit cocktail, which would typically be stirred, The Line Cocktail is shaken—aerating the liquid and adding texture and body to this refreshing drink.

INGREDIENTS

- 2 dashes Angostura® aromatic bitters
- ⅓ ounce Bénédictine
- ⅓ ounce sweet vermouth
- ⅓ ounce dry gin

GARNISH

* Crushed sweet pickled rakkyo (spring onion) or crushed pickled cocktail onion and a thin orange twist

GLASS

* Cordial

METHOD

1. Add all the ingredients to a cocktail shaker with 3 cubes of ice.
2. Shake for 15 seconds until very cold.
3. Strain into a cordial glass.
4. Garnish with crushed sweet pickled rakkyo or, if not available, a crushed pickled cocktail onion, and a thin orange twist.

If you can't source sweet pickled rakkyo (spring onion), a pickled cocktail onion will do a similar job of adding the sweet and sour salinity that gives this drink a special flourish.

PEGU CLUB

Bright, bracing, citrusy

The Pegu Club cocktail was the signature cocktail at the British officers' Pegu Club in Rangoon, Burma, now Yangon, Myanmar. The judicious use of bitters adds complexity without overwhelming the drink, while the orange bitters help to brighten the flavors. In 2005, it became the namesake of one of the most influential bars of the craft cocktail renaissance, Pegu Club in New York City, which sadly closed in 2020.

INGREDIENTS

- 2 ounces gin
- ⅔ ounce fresh lime juice
- ⅔ ounce orange curaçao
- 2 dashes Angostura® aromatic bitters
- 1 dash Angostura® orange bitters

GARNISH

* Lime wheel

GLASS

* Coupe, chilled

METHOD

1. Add all the ingredients to a cocktail shaker.
2. Add some ice and shake for 15 seconds until well chilled.
3. Strain into a chilled coupe and garnish with a lime wheel.

MARGARITA

Refreshing, citrusy, punchy

One of the earliest printed Margarita recipes is from *Esquire*, December 1953, which read, "She's from Mexico, Señores, and her name is the Margarita Cocktail—and she is lovely to look at, exciting and provocative." This simple combination of 100% agave tequila, orange liqueur, and fresh lime juice can be elevated with a couple of dashes of orange bitters. There are several plausible but no proven origins of the Margarita cocktail, but what is undisputed is that the Margarita is one of the most popular cocktails in both the United States and United Kingdom.

INGREDIENTS

- Lime wedge and flaky sea salt for the rim
- 1¾ ounces 100% agave blanco tequila
- ¾ ounce triple sec
- ¾ ounce fresh lime juice
- 2 dashes Angostura® orange bitters

GARNISH

* Lime wheel or twist

GLASS

* Coupe, chilled

METHOD

1. Half-rim the coupe with the lime wedge and flaky sea salt (see below).
2. Combine the tequila, triple sec, lime juice, and orange bitters in a cocktail shaker.
3. Half-fill with ice and shake for 15 seconds until well chilled.
4. Fine strain into the chilled and salt-rimmed coupe.
5. Garnish with a lime wheel or twist.

To half-rim a glass with salt, place a handful of flaky sea salt on a plate. Slice a wedge of lime and make a small cut into its flesh. Squeeze the lime a little and run it along the mouth of the glass. Then, roll the glass rim in the sea salt. The lime juice will ensure that the salt sticks.

LONDON CALLING

Nutty, dry, fruity

The London Calling was one of the bestsellers at Milk & Honey, a Soho speakeasy on the London cocktail scene that sadly closed in 2020. It's a gin sour that uses fino sherry to provide distinctive salty, nutty notes that are lifted by the zesty orange bitters and grapefruit garnish. Named after punk band The Clash's seminal album, this drink has risen from the underground to international fame and is now considered a modern classic.

INGREDIENTS

- 1¾ ounces gin
- ½ ounce fino sherry
- ½ ounce fresh lemon juice
- ⅓ ounce simple syrup
- 2 dashes Angostura® orange bitters

GARNISH

* Pink grapefruit twist

GLASS

* Coupe, chilled

METHOD

1. Add all the ingredients to a cocktail shaker.
2. Half-fill with ice and shake for 15 seconds until well chilled.
3. Strain into a chilled coupe.
4. Garnish with a pink grapefruit twist.

The original recipe called for a smaller measure of a higher-proof navy-strength gin, so if you have some on hand, give that a try. Some recipes call for equal measures of fino sherry, lemon juice, and simple syrup, but we've dialed back the simple syrup here. However, you can play around with the proportions depending on your palate.

JULIET AND ROMEO

Fresh, floral, herbal

A refreshing summer cocktail that also sells particularly well on Valentine's Day, a Juliet and Romeo tastes like walking through an English garden. There's plenty of rose on the nose, and on the palate there's a delicious mix of botanicals, lime, cucumber, and mint. Created at the Violet Hour, one of Chicago's first craft cocktail bars in 2007, this one's a modern classic in the making.

INGREDIENTS

- 3 slices cucumber
- 1 pinch salt
- ¾ ounce simple syrup
- 2 ounces gin
- ¾ ounce fresh lime juice
- 1 sprig fresh mint
- 1 dash rose water
- 3 dashes Angostura® aromatic bitters

GARNISH

* Fresh mint leaf

GLASS

* Coupe, chilled

METHOD

1. Add the cucumber and salt to a cocktail shaker and muddle.
2. Add the simple syrup, gin, lime juice, and mint sprig to the shaker.
3. Half-fill with ice and shake for 15 seconds until well chilled.
4. Strain into a chilled coupe.
5. Garnish with a mint leaf, add the dash of rose water on the mint leaf, then add the bitters.

This is a crowd-pleaser of a cocktail—a gin cocktail for people who think they don't like gin—try it and win over some new friends! They'll be surprised in a good way.

JOHANN GOES TO MEXICO

Smoky, spicy, citrusy

The Johann Goes to Mexico is named after the creator of Angostura, Dr. Johann Siegert. This mezcal drink is a memorable take on a Trinidad Sour, balancing the characteristic smoke of mezcal and the deep flavorful spice of bitters.

INGREDIENTS

- 1½ ounces mezcal, preferably Vida
- ½ ounce fresh lemon juice
- ½ ounce Angostura® aromatic bitters
- ½ ounce demerara syrup (see below)

GLASS

* Cordial, chilled

METHOD

1. Combine all the ingredients in a cocktail shaker.
2. Half-fill with ice and shake for 15 seconds until well chilled.
3. Double strain into a chilled cordial glass.

To make demerara syrup, combine equal measures of demerara sugar and water and heat gently in a pan until all the sugar is dissolved. Cool and strain into a sterilized glass bottle, refrigerate, and use within a month.

Since 1824
ANGOSTURA
orange bitters
INGREDIENTS: WATER,
GLYCERINE, ALCOHOL,
alc. 28.0% vol.
MANUFACTURED BY ANGOSTURA LTD.
100ml e

SPIRITED DRINKS

When serving cocktails that are heavy on the liquor with very little in the way of mixer, the quality of that base spirit is really important. These short drinks are designed for the spirit to shine. Generally, stronger drinks are stirred to chill and gently dilute without over-agitating by shaking, which can damage the delicate aromatics of the spirit.

We highlight the Martinez, a precursor to the Martini and often considered a Gin Manhattan, for its use of sweet vermouth in a gin drink. You'll also find some modern classics, such as the Oaxaca Old-Fashioned, one of the first cocktails to thrust mezcal on to the international scene, and another good agave adaptation in the Rosita, a tequila twist on the Negroni. And if your preferred spirit base is rum or whiskey, we also have you covered with a honeyed Chet Baker or a twist on a Sazerac.

A STORY IN EVERY DASH: THE MARTINI

First popularized in the 1890s, the Martini truly is the king of all cocktails. It has a cult-like following, transcending borders and generations, and it has infiltrated art, film, and literature like no other drink.

Despite what James Bond would have you believe, the Martini is a stirred cocktail. The classic Dry Martini found in *The Savoy Cocktail Book* from 1930 called for a dash of orange bitters alongside gin and vermouth. Today, our orange bitters play an essential role in brightening any modern Martini and add an exuberant burst of elegant zestiness to this classic cocktail.

MARTINI

Clean, zesty, delicious

The Martini is synonymous with old-school glamour and sophistication. Some may go so far as to say it's as American as apple pie. The closing scene of a movie is called the Martini shot, so is there a better way to celebrate a job well done?

INGREDIENTS

- 2 ounces gin
- ⅔ ounce dry vermouth
- 2 dashes Angostura® orange bitters

GARNISH

* Lemon twist or pitted green olive

GLASS

* Martini, chilled

METHOD

1. Add all the ingredients to a mixing glass.
2. Half-fill with ice and stir for 15 seconds until well chilled.
3. Strain into a chilled martini glass.
4. Garnish with a lemon twist or a green olive, as you prefer.

The secret to an excellent Martini is the temperature—the colder, the better. Fill your glass with ice before using or put it in the freezer if you can. The best bars keep half of your Martini on ice while you're sipping on the first half. Some bars, such as Del Diego in Madrid, will continually change your glass for a fresh ice-cold one while you're talking to prevent your Martini ever becoming warm. It's the little details that make this drink.

MARTINEZ

Rich, herbal, spirited

This sophisticated cocktail is a blend of a Manhattan and a Martini, but actually predates the Martini. Today, maraschino steps in to provide the sweetness and body when using a modern London dry gin, and the bitters provide depth and delicate spice. The recipe was first published in 1884 in *The Modern Bartenders' Guide* and is still well loved today.

INGREDIENTS

- 1½ ounces gin
- 1½ ounces sweet vermouth
- ¼ ounce maraschino liqueur
- 2 dashes Angostura® aromatic bitters

GARNISH

* Orange twist

GLASS

* Coupe, chilled

METHOD

1. Combine all the ingredients in a mixing glass.
2. Add some ice and stir for 15 seconds until well chilled.
3. Strain into a chilled coupe.
4. Garnish with an orange twist.

Keep your cocktail glasses in the freezer or add a little ice to chill the glass while you're preparing the drink and then discard.

ROSITA

Bittersweet, zesty, spicy

Bitter and boozy, this tequila twist on a Negroni was first published in 1974 but had a renaissance after being rediscovered by bar legend Gary "Gaz" Regan. Quite possibly a "perfect Negroni," this modern classic is much more complex than other takes, due to the split base of equal parts sweet and dry vermouth and the combination of bitters.

INGREDIENTS

- 1½ ounces reposado tequila
- ½ ounce Campari
- ½ ounce dry vermouth
- ½ ounce sweet vermouth
- 1 dash Angostura® aromatic bitters
- 1 dash Angostura® orange bitters

GARNISH

* Orange twist

GLASS

* Rocks

METHOD

1. Combine all the ingredients in a mixing glass.
2. Add some ice and stir for 20 seconds until well chilled.
3. Strain into a rocks glass with a large ice cube.
4. Garnish with an orange twist.

Gaz Regan's legendary technique for stirring Negronis with his finger has been immortalized with a life-sized stainless-steel cast of his finger as a Negroni stirrer. Buy one or simply use your own finger!

FITZGERALD

Fresh, tangy, fragrant

Named after American novelist F. Scott Fitzgerald, this twist on a gin sour with bitters and no egg white was created by bartender Dale DeGroff, who spearheaded the craft cocktail scene at the Rainbow Room in 1990s New York City. This drink would have been right at home at the legendary parties in *The Great Gatsby*.

INGREDIENTS

- 1¾ ounces gin
- ⅔ ounce simple syrup
- ½ ounce fresh lemon juice
- 2 dashes Angostura® aromatic bitters

GARNISH

* Lemon twist

GLASS

* Rocks

METHOD

1. Add all the ingredients to a mixing glass.
2. Half-fill with ice and stir for 15 seconds until well chilled.
3. Strain into a rocks glass with ice.
4. Garnish with a lemon twist.

> *This is a gin sour without the egg, so if you love that fresh egg white fluffiness, experiment with using a dry shake of the gin, lemon juice, bitters, and simple syrup to add air and texture. Then add ice and shake again before straining into a coupe.*

CHET BAKER

Velvety, honeyed, fruity

A liquid tribute to legendary jazz musician Chet Baker, this is a sweeter take on an Old-Fashioned, created at Milk & Honey in New York City. The use of rum in place of a spicier rye whiskey and the addition of honey syrup add a soft sweetness, perfect to soothe those vocal cords. Like Chet Baker's tunes, there are no unnecessary flourishes here. Simplicity is the secret to this drink's success, which makes it so easy to try at home.

INGREDIENTS

- 2 ounces aged rum
- 1 teaspoon honey syrup (see below)
- ⅓ ounce sweet vermouth
- 2 dashes Angostura® aromatic bitters

GARNISH

* Orange twist

GLASS

* Rocks

METHOD

1. Combine all the ingredients in a mixing glass.
2. Add ice and stir for 20 seconds until well chilled.
3. Strain over a large ice cube into a rocks glass.
4. Garnish with an orange twist.

To make honey syrup like a pro, dissolve three parts of the tastiest honey you can find with one part water over low heat on the stove. Once dissolved, leave it to cool.

MANDARIN SAZERAC

Citrusy, vanilla, licorice, spicy

The classic Sazerac is named after a bar in New Orleans. This twist on a Sazerac uses mandarin liqueur to add a citrus lift and complement the vanilla and woody notes in the bourbon. These flavors are then bound together by a few good dashes of bitters. The classic Sazerac dates back to 1838, and more than a century later, it was crowned the official cocktail of New Orleans.

Marco Nunes, Australia, Angostura Global Cocktail Competition winner, 2006

INGREDIENTS

- ¾ ounce La Fée NV Absinthe Verte
- Chilled water
- 1½ ounces Maker's Mark
- ½ ounce Mandarine Napoléon liqueur
- 3 dashes Angostura® aromatic bitters
- 1 teaspoon simple syrup

GARNISH

* Lemon twist and mandarin twist

GLASS

* Nick & Nora, chilled

METHOD

1. Rinse a chilled Nick & Nora glass with the absinthe and chilled water (see below).
2. Add the remaining ingredients to a cocktail shaker with ice.
3. Shake for 15 seconds until well chilled.
4. Strain into the absinthe-rinsed Nick & Nora glass.
5. Garnish with a lemon twist and mandarin twist.

To rinse a cocktail glass with absinthe and water, combine the two liquids and swirl around a chilled cocktail glass. Then discard the liquid.

OAXACA OLD-FASHIONED

Smoky, peppery, spicy

This is a riff on an Old-Fashioned using a split base of tequila and mezcal, which is actually quite old fashioned in its approach. Old-Fashioneds used to be made with all manner of spirits; it's only in the modern era that whiskey has laid claim to be the default base. This is one of the first modern classic cocktails that calls for mezcal. Within just a couple of years of its creation at New York City's Death & Co, an Old-Fashioned made with tequila and mezcal was adopted by bars internationally.

INGREDIENTS

- 1½ ounces reposado tequila
- ½ ounce mezcal
- 2 dashes Angostura® aromatic bitters
- 1 teaspoon agave nectar

GARNISH

* Flamed orange twist (see below)

GLASS

* Rocks

METHOD

1. Add all the ingredients to a rocks glass with one large ice cube.
2. Stir for 15 seconds until well chilled.
3. Garnish with a flamed orange twist.

To make a flamed orange twist, cut a 2-inch round of orange peel and hold it, skin side down, above the drink. Light a match and use it to warm the skin side of the peel. Squeeze the twist toward the match and the spritz of oil from the twist will briefly burst into flames. Then drop the flamed twist into the drink.

THE SCARLET IBIS

Cherry, herbal, smoky

The Scarlet Ibis is named after Trinidad and Tobago's national bird in a tribute to the wonderful scarlet color that the five dashes of bitters bring to the drink. The smoky whisky combines with the burnt sugar notes of the Madeira and the honeyed sweetness of yellow Chartreuse, while the ripe black cherries and bitters bring extra depth of flavor.

Andrew Griffiths, Australia, Angostura Global Cocktail Competition winner, 2011

INGREDIENTS

- 2 fresh black cherries, pitted
- 1 pinch sea salt
- 2 ounces Bunnahabhain 12 Year whisky
- ½ ounce aged Madeira
- ⅓ ounce yellow Chartreuse
- 5 dashes Angostura® aromatic bitters

GARNISH

* Drunk cherry oysters (see below)

GLASS

* Martini, chilled

METHOD

1. Muddle the cherries and salt in a large glass jug.
2. Add the remaining ingredients and let it sit to infuse.
3. Stir with large chunks of ice.
4. Strain into a chilled martini glass.
5. Garnish with drunk cherry oysters.

To make drunk cherry oysters, take the shredded cherries from the bottom of the jug and combine them with a dash of whisky and a pinch of salt.

OLD FLAME

Spicy, sweet, rich fruit

The Old Flame perfectly captures the sweet vibrancy and exuberance of Trinidad and Tobago. At its base is Angostura® 1824 rum, which boasts lovely dark fruit, vanilla, and spice notes, with heat from the chili-infused sherry and an aromatic lift from the orange bitters. It is a deceptively simple drink with layers upon layers of flavor that can be made by anyone anywhere.

Ray Letoa, New Zealand, Angostura Global Cocktail Competition winner, 2018

INGREDIENTS

- 1½ ounces Angostura® 1824 rum
- ½ ounce chili-infused Pedro Ximénez sherry (see below)
- 5 dashes Angostura® aromatic bitters
- 2 dashes Angostura® orange bitters

GARNISH

* Orange twist and a chili ganache chocolate

GLASS

* Rocks

METHOD

1. Add all the ingredients to a rocks glass.
2. Add a large ice cube and stir for 10 seconds until well chilled.
3. Garnish with the orange twist and a chili ganache chocolate.

To infuse Pedro Ximénez sherry with chili, cut 2 fresh red chilies and leave them to infuse in 13½ ounces of sherry for 24 hours at room temperature. Strain and bottle.

TWIN CITIES

Rich, fruity, soft spice

The Twin Cities was created for Dead Rabbit's 2022 taproom menu and uses a fig leaf–infused blend of Irish and American whiskey, Keeper's Heart, which is round, fruity, and spicy. The fig infusion works well with the coconut and vanilla notes from the ex-bourbon barrels the whiskey was aged in, and apricot brightens the nutty tones. Essentially a riff on a Manhattan with an Irish twist, this subs rye with softer Irish American whiskey.

INGREDIENTS

- 1⅔ ounces fig leaf–infused Keeper's Heart Irish + American Whiskey (see below)
- ½ ounce Pierre Ferrand 1840 cognac
- ¼ ounce Giffard Abricot du Roussillon apricot liqueur
- 1 ounce Cocchi Vermouth di Torino
- ½ teaspoon verjus blanc
- 2 dashes Angostura® cocoa bitters

GLASS

* Nick & Nora

METHOD

1. Add all the ingredients to a mixing glass.
2. Half-fill with ice and stir for 15 seconds until well chilled.
3. Strain into a Nick & Nora glass.

To make fig leaf–infused Keeper's Heart Irish + American Whiskey, combine one 750-milliliter bottle of the whiskey, ½ ounce fresh fig leaves, and ½ ounce dried fig leaves in a container with a tight-fitting lid. Steep for 2 hours at room temperature before straining and storing in a sterilized glass bottle.

THE HOUSE OF ANGOSTURA
BY APPOINTMENT TO HER MAJESTY QUEEN ELIZABETH II MANUFACTURERS OF ANGOSTURA® aromatic bitters ANGOSTURA LIMITED
ANGOSTURA
aromatic bitters
44.7% alc./vol.
alc. 44.7% vol.
200 ml
PRODUCT OF TRINIDAD & TOBAGO

★

I'M NOT DRINKING, BUT MAKE IT DELICIOUS

Not drinking does not mean you have to miss out. This chapter will help you prepare alcohol-free drinks as delicious as their full-strength counterparts. All the recipes here have been compiled with the same creativity, care, and attention as the rest of the book and contain less than 0.05% ABV.

You'll find alcohol-free twists on classic cocktails and drinks you'll recognize, as well as innovative concoctions. If you're a fan of a Negroni, try our No-groni. If a creamy Piña Colada is more your speed, check out the Nut Ah Colada. If you're looking to celebrate, try the Winter 75, an alcohol-free twist on a French icon!

A STORY IN EVERY DASH: THE LEMON, LIME, AND BITTERS

Australia lays claim to first discovering the refreshing delight that comes with combining lemon, lime, and bitters.

Bitters-based refreshers were already popular in Victorian England when Carlos Siegert, son of the founder of Angostura, visited Australia in 1879 as part of a promotional tour. But it was Australia that added the lime to the mix.

Angostura® lemon, lime & bitters is the original adult nonalcoholic cocktail, and a reported 100 million are served in Australian bars each year. It's traditional to enjoy the drink after a round of golf, although these days it is more likely to be enjoyed while watching a game of cricket or chilling on the beach or at a barbecue.

Australia's overwhelming adoption of bitters mixed with lemon, lime, and soda inspired Angostura to bottle this refreshing combination in 2007, and later to create the Chill line of vibrant, modern bitters-based refreshers.

LEMON, LIME, AND BITTERS

Citrusy, tangy, refreshing

This drink is the perfect marriage of the tart sweetness of a lemon-lime soda with the intricate flavor profile of bitters. Lemon, Lime, and Bitters is affectionately known by some as LLB, or "Lime Like a Boss" in Trinidad. Lime is not just a fruit in Trinidad, it's a term that means to party or chill with friends.

INGREDIENTS

- 1 tablespoon fresh lime juice
- 8½ ounces lemon-lime soda
- 3–4 dashes Angostura® aromatic bitters

GARNISH

* Lime wedge

GLASS

* Highball

METHOD

1. Fill a highball glass full of ice.
2. Squeeze in the fresh lime juice and top with the lemon-lime soda.
3. Add the bitters.
4. Stir gently and garnish with a lime wedge.

The Angostura® Chill line of bitters-based refreshers comes in a few different flavors, including Blood Orange & Bitters and Caribbean Sorrel (hibiscus) & Bitters. Experiment with your favorite refreshing flavor and add club soda, lime, and bitters to create your own variation.

WINTER 75

Citrusy, spicy, effervescent

This elegant sparkling blend of citrus and warming winter spice topped with alcohol-free sparkling wine is ideal for holiday celebrations. This zero-proof twist on a classic French 75 by the queen of low-and no-alcohol cocktails, Camille Vidal, hits with remarkable precision. The French 75 is a classic celebratory drink, traditionally served on New Year's Eve in France, where it is simply called the *Soixante-quinze.*

Camille Vidal (@mindfullycami at @lamaisonwellness)

INGREDIENTS

- ½ ounce allspice syrup
- ½ ounce fresh lemon juice
- 2 dashes Angostura® orange bitters
- Alcohol-free sparkling wine to top

GARNISH

* Orange twist

GLASS

* Champagne flute

METHOD

1. Combine the allspice syrup and lemon juice in a Champagne flute and stir.
2. Add the bitters.
3. Top with alcohol-free sparkling wine and garnish with an orange twist.

Serve the sparkling wine ice-cold to retain those beautiful bubbles for longer.

FRUITY BUCK

Bright, tangy, vibrant

The founder of Milk & Honey, Sasha Petraske, always said that in order to make a great mocktail, simply double the measurements of the nonalcoholic ingredients of a cocktail. By doing this, you'll have made a fantastic and versatile base that you can tweak and twist to make a nonalcoholic drink that truly suits your taste. What spin would you put on this fresh, tangy, and fruity drink?

INGREDIENTS

- 1 ounce fresh pineapple juice
- ½ ounce fresh lime juice
- ½ ounce fresh lemon juice
- 1 teaspoon agave syrup
- 2 dashes Angostura® aromatic bitters
- 3 ounces club soda

GLASS

* Collins

METHOD

1. Combine all the ingredients, except the club soda, in a cocktail shaker.
2. Add some ice and shake for 15 seconds until well chilled.
3. Pour into a Collins glass filled with ice and top with the club soda.

GREEN MIND COLLINS

Fresh, herbal, citrusy

A great Dry January drink, this is a refreshing, biting blend of celery syrup and lemon and apple juices with a couple dashes of bitters to add depth and bind the flavors together, all topped with soda. A twist on a Tom Collins without the gin, it's thirst-quenching, full of flavor, and ideal for when you need a clear head.

Camille Vidal (@mindfullycami at @lamaisonwellness)

INGREDIENTS

- ¾ ounce fresh lemon juice
- 1¾ ounces fresh apple juice
- 1 teaspoon celery syrup
- 2 dashes Angostura® aromatic bitters
- Club soda to top

GARNISH

* Apple fan (see below)

GLASS

* Collins

METHOD

1. Fill a Collins glass with ice.
2. Add the lemon and apple juices, celery syrup, and bitters.
3. Stir gently.
4. Top with club soda and garnish with an apple fan.

To make an apple fan, slice an apple in half from top to bottom and remove the core. Lay one half, cut side down, on a chopping board and cut into thin slices. Remove the first slice, then take 3 or 5 apple slices (odd numbers look better) and fan them out from the top. If necessary, use a cocktail skewer to hold the fan in place.

SOBER SUMMER CUP

Fruity, refreshing, fragrant

This is an alcohol-free twist on a Pimm's No. 1 cup, a refreshing easily batched mocktail that signals the start of summer in England and is synonymous with Wimbledon. A healthy measure of fresh lemon juice coupled with dashes of bitters provide the tartness and spicy depth of flavor without the need for alcohol. The Victorians used to blend fruit and spices in a homemade punch-style summer drink, garnished with fresh fruit to make a summery fruit cup.

INGREDIENTS

- 4 fresh mint leaves
- 3½ ounces lemon-lime soda
- 6 cucumber slices
- 2 fresh strawberries, quartered
- 2 lemon wedges
- 1¾ ounces ginger ale
- ¾ ounce cola
- ¾ ounce fresh orange juice
- 1 tablespoon fresh lemon juice
- 2 dashes Angostura® aromatic bitters

GARNISH

* Cucumber slices, fresh strawberry halves, fresh mint leaves, and lemon wheel

GLASS

* Highball

METHOD

1. Muddle the mint leaves in a highball glass.
2. Add half of the lemon-lime soda and the rest of the ingredients.
3. Stir to combine.
4. Chill in the fridge for 3 hours to allow the flavors to combine.
5. To serve, add some ice and the remaining lemon-lime soda.
6. Garnish with cucumber slices, strawberry halves, mint leaves, and a lemon wheel.

The Sober Summer Cup is designed to be shared, so simply multiply the ingredients by the number of guests and serve in a glass jug with a big wooden spoon to allow for a quick stir before pouring each glass.

4-WAY CITRUS SHRUB

Citrusy, fresh, vibrant

This is a twist on a Lemon, Lime, and Bitters (page 126) that is all about using leftover citrus peels and husks. We've used lemons, limes, grapefruits, and oranges, but you can use any citrus fruit you'd like. This drink taps into the trends for zero-waste and alcohol-free cocktails, so it's a real feel-good drink.

Rohan Massie, Australia, 2021

INGREDIENTS

- 1 ounce 4-way citrus shrub (see below)
- 3–4 dashes Angostura® aromatic bitters
- Club soda to top

GARNISH

* Citrus wedge

GLASS

* Collins

METHOD

1. Combine the shrub and bitters in a Collins glass over ice.
2. Top with the club soda and garnish with a citrus wedge.

To make the 4-way citrus shrub, take 1 handful of leftover citrus peels and husks. Combine with 2⅔ cups superfine sugar, give it all a light massage to get the oils flowing, and leave, covered, overnight. The next day, add 25½ ounces hot water (approximately at the temperature you would drink tea) and stir to dissolve the sugar. Strain out the fruit and add 1¾ ounces Chardonnay vinegar to provide acidity. Pour the shrub into a sterilized glass bottle and seal. Cool, then keep in the fridge for up to 2 weeks.

NUT AH COLADA

Tropical, rich, creamy

The Piña Colada sings of summer days—one sip and your mind immediately escapes to a beach. No need to miss out if you're not drinking, this alcohol-free version includes a little peanut butter along with coconut cream and the earthy richness of cocoa bitters to provide depth of flavor.

INGREDIENTS

- 4 dashes Angostura® cocoa bitters
- 3 ounces fresh pineapple juice
- 1 teaspoon creamy peanut butter
- 1 ounce coconut cream
- 1 ounce whole milk

GARNISH

* Edible flower

GLASS

* Highball

METHOD

1. Add all the ingredients to a cocktail shaker.
2. Add some ice and shake for 20 seconds until well chilled.
3. Double strain into a highball glass filled with ice.
4. Garnish with an edible flower.

Use creamy peanut butter instead of crunchy for a smooth, rich, sweet depth to this drink.

AMARETTI SOUR

Almondy, sweet, sour, velvety

This Amaretto Sour without the alcohol comes from the smart folk at Lyre's Spirit Co., who have figured out how to create sober versions of many of our favorite full-strength spirits. This is a delicious, short, grown-up drink that offers a fancy experience for those not drinking. The Amaretto Sour came of age in the 1970s.

INGREDIENTS

- 2½ ounces Lyre's Amaretti
- ½ ounce fresh lemon juice
- 1 teaspoon simple syrup
- ⅓ ounce egg white
- 3 dashes Angostura® aromatic bitters

GARNISH

* Lemon wedge and brandied cherry

GLASS

* Rocks

METHOD

1. Add all the ingredients to a shaker.
2. Fill with ice and shake hard and fast for 20 seconds.
3. Strain into a rocks glass.
4. Add fresh ice and garnish with a lemon wedge and brandied cherry.

Vegan? Use aquafaba in place of egg white. To make aquafaba, drain a can of chickpeas and, using a handheld electric mixer, whip up the liquid for 3–6 minutes until it forms soft peaks. There you have it: a vegan, egg-free alternative to egg white that provides the same lovely texture in sours.

NO-GRONI

Bittersweet, herbal, citrusy

A classic aperitif (from the Latin *aperire*, to open), a Negroni is designed to open your appetite before dinner. But you don't need alcohol to help stimulate your hunger. The No-groni will do the same job and tastes just as delicious. This is probably one of the few new classic alcohol-free cocktails.

INGREDIENTS

- 1 ounce Seedlip Spice 94 or an alcohol-free gin
- 1 ounce Giffard Apéritif Syrup
- 1 ounce Lyre's Apéritif Rosso
- 2 dashes Angostura® orange bitters
- 2 dashes Angostura® aromatic bitters

GARNISH

* Orange twist

GLASS

* Rocks

METHOD

1. Add all the ingredients to a mixing glass.
2. Half-fill with ice and stir for 15 seconds until well chilled.
3. Strain into a rocks glass filled with ice.
4. Garnish with an orange twist.

This is a great drink to batch in advance and simply pour when ready to serve for minimal fuss and maximum flavor when hosting.

OBELIX

Fruity, fresh, effervescent

This is a bold, mesmerizing blend of tangy fruit, bitters, and soda. The intense bold botanicals of the bitters shine through alongside fresh pineapple and lime juice, raspberry syrup, and a good splash of Schweppes Russchian Pink Soda.

Antonia Lo Casto, Italy, Angostura Global Cocktail Challenge winner, 2011

INGREDIENTS

- ⅔ ounce fresh pineapple juice
- 1 teaspoon lime syrup
- 1 teaspoon raspberry syrup
- ⅔ ounce Schweppes Russchian Pink Soda (see below)
- 3 dashes Angostura® aromatic bitters

GARNISH

* Apple slice, lime wheel, orange twist, and pineapple leaves

GLASS

* Collins

METHOD

1. Combine all the ingredients in a Collins glass.
2. Add ice.
3. Stir gently.
4. Garnish with an apple slice, lime wheel, orange twist, and pineapple leaves.

If you're struggling to find Schweppes Russchian Pink Soda, which includes a tantalizing mix of red berries, hibiscus, and carrot and is not widely available in the United States, try a good-quality sparkling pink lemonade and half the measure of raspberry syrup.

BY APPOINTMENT TO HER
MAJESTY QUEEN ELIZABETH II
MANUFACTURERS OF
ANGOSTURA® aromatic bitters
ANGOSTURA LIMITED
ANGOSTURA
aromatic bitters
44.7% alc./vol.
alc. 44.7% vol.
200 ml
PRODUCT OF TRINIDAD & TOBAGO

APERITIFS

Aperitifs are drinks designed to open the appetite, ideal to enjoy before or with food. They often include ingredients with a lighter ABV, such as vermouths, sherries, bitter liqueurs, or the bourbon highball. They are also very well diluted with a 4:1 or 5:1 ratio of spirit to mixers to allow a light, refreshing start to proceedings before the stomach is suitably lined.

Italian aperitivo culture has exploded globally in recent years, and the Negroni has gone from a bartender secret to worldwide phenomenon. Here, we've got a great twist on the Negroni in the form of a Cacao Negroni using a rose-scented gin.

Different countries have different drinks that are traditional as aperitifs. In Spain, for example, vermouth is a popular aperitif. Frequently enjoyed simply on the rocks or in a special local concoction often involving a splash of gin and club soda, the Media Combinación pays homage to this rustic style of Spanish aperitif.

A STORY IN EVERY DASH: THE PINK GIN

One of the earliest cocktails to be made with bitters was the Pink Gin. It was created by sailors who started drinking bitters to combat stomach ailments. However, they soon discovered that adding a dash or two of bitters to their daily ration of Plymouth gin made a delicious drink.

The Pink Gin cocktail is traditionally served warm or at room temperature and undiluted as a testament to its nautical origins, as there would not be ice readily available aboard ships in the 19th century.

PINK GIN

Aromatic, citrusy, herbal

The Pink Gin was created out of necessity by Royal Navy officers who were looking for something to sweeten bitters prescribed to settle their stomachs and quell seasickness while at sea. The marriage of botanical gin and aromatic bitters took place in the mid-1820s, long before the Gin and Tonic became a thing.

INGREDIENTS

- 2 ounces gin
- 3 dashes Angostura® aromatic bitters

GARNISH

* Lemon twist

GLASS

* Coupe, chilled

METHOD

1. In a mixing glass, stir both ingredients with ice to chill.
2. Strain into a chilled coupe.
3. Express the oils from the lemon twist over the cocktail and use the twist to garnish.

While traditionally served warm or at room temperature, there are two ways to serve a Pink Gin. You can prepare it as described above, or you might prefer to coat a chilled glass with a few dashes of bitters swirled around before adding the gin.

VIEJÍSIMO ADONIS

Opulent, rich, dried fruit

This "very old Adonis" is a spectacle from 1862 Dry Bar—a bar in Madrid named after the year that Jerry Thomas's first bartender guide was published. The Adonis is the original low-alcohol cocktail that is often "thrown," a traditional Spanish technique used to aerate and amplify aromatics in wine-based ingredients such as sherry and vermouth. It was created around 1885 by Joseph F. McKone to celebrate a popular Broadway show called *Adonis*.

Alberto Martinez, 1862 Dry Bar, Spain, 2017

INGREDIENTS

- 1½ ounces Lustau VORS amontillado
- 1½ ounces Lustau red vermouth
- 1 teaspoon Lustau East India Solera cream sherry
- 2 dashes Angostura® orange bitters

GARNISH

* Pitted green olive and orange twist

GLASS

* Nick & Nora

METHOD

1. Assemble your cocktail in one tin of your two-piece shaker. Add ice and hold a strainer on top to keep it from falling out.
2. Hold that tin (the "throwing" one) with one hand over your head. This hand will stay still.
3. Hold the other tin (the "receiving" one) with the other hand as far down as possible. Now you are ready.
4. Keeping your throwing hand above your head, bring the receiving tin up closer and start pouring. During this pouring, slowly lower the receiving tin as far down as you can until all the liquid has been transferred.
5. Repeat this process four or five times, then pour into a Nick & Nora glass.
6. Garnish with a green olive and an orange twist.

This is a great cocktail to batch in advance and then throw around to liven up before serving.

BAMBOO

Bone-dry, savory, citrusy

The Bamboo was created by bartender Louis Eppinger in San Francisco as early as 1886. The 50:50 ratio of dry vermouth to fino sherry makes it a beautifully balanced, elegant, and complex cocktail. The Bamboo is the second great sherry-vermouth drink inspired by the success of the Manhattan and bartenders' desire to create a lower-proof drink.

INGREDIENTS

- 1½ ounces fino sherry
- 1½ ounces dry vermouth
- 1 dash Angostura® aromatic bitters
- 1 dash Angostura® orange bitters

GARNISH

* Lemon twist

GLASS

* Coupe, chilled

METHOD

1. Add all the ingredients to a mixing glass.
2. Half-fill with ice and stir for 15 seconds until well chilled.
3. Strain into a chilled coupe and garnish with a lemon twist.

Sherry is delicious and incredibly good value. It's wonderful in cocktails and with food. The salinity of a fino gives the wine a savory umami note, which means it can stand up to big complex foods that would cause some wines to struggle. It works really well with sushi or mushroom dishes, and its tanginess can stand up to olives and cured meats. Once opened, fino is best refrigerated and consumed within a few days.

BOOTHBY COCKTAIL

Decadent, rich, aromatic

An eponymous cocktail, the Boothby Cocktail was created by San Francisco bartender William T. Boothby, known as "Cocktail Bill." The Boothby is essentially a Manhattan Royale: rye, sweet vermouth, and bitters lengthened with Champagne. It's been around since at least 1891 and is still being enjoyed today.

INGREDIENTS

- 2 ounces rye whiskey or bourbon
- 1 ounce sweet vermouth
- 2 dashes Angostura® orange bitters
- 1 dash Angostura® aromatic bitters
- 1 ounce Champagne

GARNISH

* Brandied cherry

GLASS

* Coupe, chilled

METHOD

1. Combine the whiskey, vermouth, and bitters in a mixing glass.
2. Half-fill with ice and stir for 15 seconds until well chilled.
3. Strain into a chilled coupe.
4. Top with the Champagne and garnish with a brandied cherry.

Using rye gives more of a crisp, spicy bite, while bourbon leads to a softer drink.

TRINITY

Bittersweet, aromatic

The Trinity is so-called for the trio of French dry vermouth, Italian sweet vermouth, and three dashes of bitters. It was featured in Angostura's 1924 *Centenary Gift Book of Cocktails and Other Recipes*, published to celebrate our 100th anniversary. It's perhaps not a classic anymore, but maybe it's time for a revival!

INGREDIENTS

- 1 ounce gin
- 1 ounce French dry vermouth
- 1 ounce Italian sweet vermouth
- 3 dashes Angostura® aromatic bitters

GARNISH

* Lemon twist

GLASS

* Rocks

METHOD

1. Combine all the ingredients in a rocks glass.
2. Add ice and stir gently.
3. Garnish with a lemon twist.

> *Keep your vermouth in the fridge. Vermouth is a fortified wine, which means that, once you open the bottle, exposure to air or more oxygen causes a reaction that changes the flavor profile . . . and not for the better. The best way to slow this process is to refrigerate your vermouth once opened. This will help it stay vibrant and fresher for longer.*

MEDIA COMBINACIÓN

Bittersweet, fragrant, citrusy

This rustic Spanish drink mixes vermouth and gin (or any other spirit), topped with any number of garnishes. It was born in an era when resources were scarce and people wanted an aperitif cocktail that made use of the plentiful resources at the time: gin and vermouth.

INGREDIENTS

- 2 ounces Spanish red vermouth
- 1 ounce London dry gin
- ¼ ounce orange curaçao
- 2 dashes Angostura® aromatic bitters

GARNISH

* Orange twist and a pitted green olive

GLASS

* Rocks

METHOD

1. Add all the ingredients to a rocks glass full of ice.
2. Stir gently.
3. Express the oils from the orange twist into the drink.
4. Place the orange twist in the glass.
5. Garnish with the green olive.

THE CHARMER

Herbal, sweet, tangy

This drink is how Daniyel Jones charmed himself into a job as Angostura ambassador after wowing judges with his freestyle cocktail at our Global Cocktail Competition in 2013. The combination of rum, Bénédictine liqueur, sherry vinegar, and lime juice is balanced by honey and five dashes of bitters. The foam finish makes this drink fancy. It is tantalizing on the tongue but deceptively simple to make.

Daniyel Jones, Trinidad and Tobago, Angostura Global Cocktail Challenge winner, 2013, now Angostura ambassador

INGREDIENTS

- 1½ ounces Angostura® 5-year-old rum
- ⅔ ounce Bénédictine liqueur
- ⅓ ounce sherry vinegar
- ⅓ ounce fresh lime juice
- 1 teaspoon organic honey
- 5 dashes Angostura® aromatic bitters

GARNISH

* Bay leaf foam (see below)

GLASS

* Nick & Nora, chilled

METHOD

1. Add all the ingredients to a cocktail shaker.
2. Half-fill with ice and shake for 10–15 seconds until chilled.
3. Strain and serve into a chilled Nick & Nora glass.
4. Garnish with the bay leaf foam.

To make bay leaf foam, add 4 egg whites, 3 ounces Angostura® aromatic bitters, 3 ounces honey infused with bay leaves for 14 days, 2 tablespoons lemon juice, and 2 ounces water to an iSi Whipper, then cap and shake to mix. Charge the iSi Whipper twice, shaking between charges. Chill for at least 1 hour before use.

BOURBON HIGHBALL

Light, zesty, refreshing

This refreshingly simple combination of bourbon, club soda, and a dash of orange bitters is the perfect aperitif for whiskey fans. Served ice cold, this is a great pre-dinner drink and also has enough acidity to accompany fatty fried foods. The highball is an aperitif that originated in the United Kingdom, was popularized in the United States, and perfected into an artform in Japan.

INGREDIENTS

- 1⅓ ounces bourbon
- 4 ounces club soda
- 1 dash Angostura® orange bitters

GARNISH

* Orange twist

GLASS

* Highball

METHOD

1. Add the bourbon to a highball glass filled with ice.
2. Top with the club soda.
3. Add the bitters and gently stir.
4. Garnish with an orange twist.

Chill the club soda and pour over the back of a spoon along the side of the glass, avoiding direct contact with the ice to help retain the bubbles in the soda.

CUBAN CHAWARI

Fragrant, fresh, spicy

Chawari means "cut with tea" and is a variation on another aperitif, a Mizuwari, which means "cut with water." It's a traditional way to enjoy a whisky or shochu in Japan. In this iteration, rum is paired with tea and spiked with flavorful accents. It was created at Kwãnt Mayfair in London, which attracts the best in the cocktail industry from all over the world.

Gento Torigata, Kwãnt Mayfair, United Kingdom, 2023

INGREDIENTS

- 1⅓ ounces Caribbean spiced rum
- 2 ounces Taiwanese black tea (see below)
- 1 teaspoon oloroso sherry
- 1 scant teaspoon agave nectar
- 1 dash Muyu Jasmine Verte liqueur
- 2 dashes Angostura® aromatic bitters

GLASS

* Nick & Nora

METHOD

1. Combine all the ingredients in a mixing glass.
2. Half-fill with ice and stir for 15 seconds until well chilled.
3. Pour into a Nick & Nora glass with a large ice cube.

Brew the tea with a ratio of 1 ounce tea leaves to 3 ounces hot water (195°F) for 5 minutes, then strain and cool before use.

CACAO NEGRONI

Bittersweet, rose, dark chocolate

The Negroni has found new fame in recent years, and this rose version uses a double measure of South African Bayab rose water gin, rose vermouth, cacao-infused Campari and a couple of dashes of cocoa bitters. The Negroni dates to the 1920s when Count Camillo Negroni ordered his Americano with gin rather than club soda.

INGREDIENTS

- 2 ounces Bayab African Rose Water gin
- 1 ounce rose vermouth
- 1 ounce cacao-infused Campari (see below)
- 2 dashes Angostura® cocoa bitters

GARNISH

* Orange twist

GLASS

* Rocks

METHOD

1. Combine all the ingredients in a rocks glass.
2. Add a large ice cube.
3. Stir for 15 seconds until well chilled.
4. Garnish with an orange twist.

To make the cacao-infused Campari, simply add 1 tablespoon of fresh cacao pods to a bottle of Campari and leave overnight. Remove the pods and strain.

cocoa bitters
THE HOUSE OF ANGOSTURA
ANGOSTURA
cocoa
bitters
A DISTINCTIVE EXPRESSION
EXPERTLY CRAFTED WITH FINE
TRINITARIO COCOA NIBS

DIGESTIFS

After-dinner cocktails were traditionally drinks that would help you digest your meal and would often include any number of bitter liqueurs, herbs, and spices thought to help calm the stomach. The classy Champs-Élysées is a classic post-dinner drink with cognac and herbal green Chartreuse, lemon, bitters, and a touch of sugar.

The Bijou or Doctor's Orders could easily replace dessert and provide the same sweet lift often appreciated at the end of a meal.

If you're a fan of a cheese board, there is the perfect Manhattan, made with a British brandy and garnished with a slice of pecorino.

Coffee is a big post-dinner occasion, and here we have three coffee-based cocktails: a rich bitter chocolate take on an Espresso Martini; a Mr. Brown, an invigorating blend of bourbon and coffee; and a Café Trinidad, the island's answer to an Irish coffee.

A STORY IN EVERY DASH: THE ESPRESSO MARTINI

The Espresso Martini is a modern classic cocktail created by the godfather of the London cocktail scene, Dick Bradsell. The creation of the drink is part of modern cocktail folklore: Around 1983, a budding supermodel requested a drink that would simultaneously wake her up and, ahem, mess her up.

The Espresso Martini has experienced a revival in recent years—it was one of the most ordered cocktails in US bars in 2023. Using fresh espresso and a long hard shake is the best way to create the signature froth, which takes a good amount of work during a busy bar shift.

Nowadays, there are even more choices in terms of quality coffee liqueurs and cocoa bitters to accent this modern classic. The signature three coffee beans atop an Espresso Martini signify health, wealth, and happiness.

ESPRESSO MARTINI

Rich, bitter, sweet

This was originally known as a Vodka Espresso and later as the Pharmaceutical Stimulant before finally being crowned the Espresso Martini. It seemingly fails to go out of fashion, as coffee and spirits are a winning combination. A true modern classic, the drink is replicated around the world and is a true bar call. Whether it's on menus or not, people will ask for it!

INGREDIENTS

- 1½ ounces vodka
- ½ ounce coffee liqueur
- 1 ounce freshly brewed espresso
- ½ ounce simple syrup
- 6 dashes Angostura® cocoa bitters

GARNISH

* 3 coffee beans

GLASS

* Coupe, chilled

METHOD

1. Pour all the ingredients into a cocktail shaker.
2. Add ice and shake vigorously for 20 seconds until nice and frothy.
3. Strain into a chilled coupe and garnish with the coffee beans.

The trick to a good Espresso Martini is in the frothy head. For this, you need to use a good-quality espresso that will have the right oils and shake it vigorously, then let the foam settle in your glass before you garnish.

BIJOU

Bright, sweet, herbaceous

A real jewel of a drink, Bijou includes a trio of ingredients that shine like gems with an accent of orange bitters. Bijou means "jewel" in French and is inspired by the hues of the drink's three main components: gin for diamond, sweet vermouth for ruby, and green Chartreuse for emerald. One of the earliest cocktails to call for orange bitters, the Bijou cocktail is a Harry Johnson creation from 1900.

INGREDIENTS

- 1½ ounces gin
- ⅔ ounce sweet vermouth
- ⅔ ounce green Chartreuse
- 2 dashes Angostura® orange bitters

GARNISH

* Lemon twist

GLASS

* Coupe, chilled

METHOD

1. Combine all the ingredients in a mixing glass.
2. Add ice and stir for 15 seconds until well chilled.
3. Strain into a chilled coupe.
4. Garnish with a lemon twist.

CHAMPS-ÉLYSÉES

Light, citrusy, herbaceous

Named after the famous Parisian avenue, this is an elegant variation on a Sidecar that uses herbal green Chartreuse in place of zesty curaçao. This substitution is, as the French would say, a *triomphe*! While the recipe was first published in 1925, the team at Milk & Honey in New York City had a hand in reviving this classic.

INGREDIENTS

- 1½ ounces cognac
- ½ ounce green Chartreuse
- ⅔ ounce fresh lemon juice
- ½ ounce simple syrup
- 3–4 dashes Angostura® aromatic bitters

GARNISH

* Lemon twist

GLASS

* Coupe or Nick & Nora, chilled

METHOD

1. Combine all the ingredients in a cocktail shaker with ice.
2. Shake well.
3. Strain into a chilled coupe or Nick & Nora glass.
4. Garnish with a lemon twist.

Use a young VS cognac for more of those fragrant, floral fruity notes and not an XO cognac, which will have too complex a flavor profile that could overpower this drink.

BLACK MANHATTAN

Bittersweet, aromatic, strong

This is an inspired simple switch. In a Black Manhattan, sweet vermouth is subbed for the richer, bittersweet herbal amaro, which bartenders in the United States were getting a taste for back in 2005. This is a really easy, intensely flavored drink for a professional or home bartender.

INGREDIENTS

- 2 ounces rye whiskey
- 1 ounce amaro
- 1 dash Angostura® aromatic bitters
- 1 dash Angostura® orange bitters

GARNISH

* Brandied cherry

GLASS

* Coupe, chilled

METHOD

1. Combine all the ingredients in a mixing glass.
2. Add ice and stir well.
3. Strain into chilled coupe.
4. Garnish with a brandied cherry or two.

This drink was originally made with Averna amaro, but there are so many different styles of amaro, play around with what you have at home and see what difference it makes.

MR. BROWN

Silky, strong, indulgent

Mr. Brown is the perfect nightcap—a blend of bourbon and coffee liqueur with a touch of vanilla syrup and a dash of aromatic and orange bitters. The name is inspired by the Quentin Tarantino film *Reservoir Dogs*, which includes a particular scene that anyone working in hospitality will remember well. Created by Frankie Marshall at the Clover Club in New York City, this will no doubt become a modern classic due to its simplicity but complex layers of flavor.

INGREDIENTS

- 2 ounces bourbon
- ⅔ ounce coffee liqueur, preferably Heering
- 1 teaspoon vanilla syrup (see below)
- 1 dash Angostura® aromatic bitters
- 1 dash Angostura® orange bitters

GARNISH

* Orange twist

GLASS

* Rocks

METHOD

1. Combine all the ingredients in a mixing glass.
2. Add some ice and stir for 45 seconds until well chilled.
3. Strain into a rocks glass over a large ice cube.
4. Garnish with an orange twist.

To make your own vanilla syrup, combine 1 split vanilla pod with equal measures of water and sugar in a saucepan over medium heat, then stir until sugar has dissolved. Remove from the heat and let it cool. Remove the vanilla pod and store the syrup in a sterilized glass bottle, where it will keep for around 2 weeks.

CAFÉ TRINIDAD

Sweet, rich, coffee

This is a Trinidad twist on an Irish coffee. Instead of whiskey, there are several dashes of orange and cocoa bitters added to a sweet, chilled coffee with that signature cool, cream float. The result is a less boozy but equally flavorful drink perfect after a meal. Trinidadians love adding bitters to their morning brew, so this is a very Trini take on an after-dinner drink.

INGREDIENTS

- 2 ounces chilled espresso
- ¾ ounce demerara syrup (see page 96)
- 2 dashes Angostura® orange bitters
- 6 dashes Angostura® cocoa bitters
- Heavy cream, slightly whipped

GARNISH

* Grated nutmeg and an edible flower (optional)

GLASS

* Champagne flute, chilled

METHOD

1. Add all the ingredients to a cocktail shaker, except the heavy cream.
2. Shake with some ice.
3. Strain into a chilled Champagne flute.
4. Float the cream on top (see below).
5. Garnish with a dusting of grated nutmeg and an edible flower, if using.

To help the heavy cream float, whip the cream just a little so it has a thick texture, but not too much, then pour over the back of a spoon.

DOCTOR'S ORDERS

Fresh, fruity, pungent

This could easily be a delicious liquid dessert—beautifully balanced, sweet and fruity with freshness and texture. This drink celebrates simplicity and technique. Creatively pairing simple flavors and classic techniques can produce a perfect drink without the need for any fancy bar equipment.

Rohan Massie, Australia, Angostura Global Cocktail Competition finalist, 2020

INGREDIENTS

- 1¾ ounces Angostura® 5-year-old rum
- 10 fresh basil leaves
- ⅔ ounce strawberry cordial (see below)
- 1⅓ ounces fresh mandarin juice
- 1 ounce coconut milk
- 1 teaspoon fresh lime juice
- 2 dashes Angostura® orange bitters

GARNISH

* Fresh basil sprigs and freeze-dried mandarin segments

GLASS

* Pearl diver

METHOD

1. Add all the ingredients to a cocktail shaker.
2. Add some ice cubes.
3. Short shake for 5 seconds.
4. Double strain over crushed ice in a pearl diver glass.
5. Garnish with basil sprigs and freeze-dried mandarin segments.

To make a strawberry cordial, combine 10½ ounces of fresh strawberries with ⅔ cup superfine sugar, the juice of 1 lemon, and 6½ ounces of water. Bring to a boil, then turn down the heat and simmer for 15 minutes. Leave to cool for 1 hour. Mash the strawberries with the back of a spoon and strain through a fine mesh sieve. Pour the cordial into a sterilized glass bottle and seal. Cool, then keep in the fridge for up to 2 weeks.

AMARO BANK BURST

Rich, refreshing, bittersweet

This cocktail is inspired by the immense power of an agitated river bursting its bank, as witnessed by bartender Marv Cunningham when Tropical Storm Karen hit Trinidad in 2019. This culinary cocktail uses distinctive ingredients found in a kitchen, like spicy lemongrass and tamarind, which can also be used to delicious effect in a drink.

Marv Cunningham, The Bahamas, Angostura Global Cocktail Competition winner, 2020

INGREDIENTS

- 1 ounce amaro di Angostura®
- 1 ounce Angostura® 1919 rum
- 5 ounces tamarind pulp
- 5 ounces spicy lemongrass syrup (see below)
- 1 ounce fresh coconut water
- 2 dashes Angostura® orange bitters
- 5 dashes Angostura® aromatic bitters

GARNISH

* Lemongrass stalk and an edible flower

GLASS

* Highball

METHOD

1. Combine all the ingredients in a cocktail shaker.
2. Add some ice and shake for 15 seconds until well chilled.
3. Strain into a highball glass.
4. Add some ice to serve and garnish with a lemongrass stalk and an edible flower.

Unusually, the modifying agent used here is tamarind pulp, which provides a rich acidic and tart backbone to the drink, while the spicy lemongrass syrup provides the sweet element. To make spicy lemongrass syrup, add a lemongrass stalk and a fresh red chili to 4 ounces of water and ½ cup of sugar. Put over low heat and stir until the sugar is all dissolved. Set aside and leave to cool for 1 hour. Strain into a sterilized glass bottle and seal. Refrigerate and use within a week.

CHEESE BOARD MANHATTAN

Bittersweet, fragrant, tangy

Is cheese served before or after dessert in your house? Either way, this cocktail complements your cheese board as perfectly as grapes and jam. It uses a British brandy, a grape-based spirit in place of whiskey, and a touch of quince jam for a sweet, floral twist on the classic Manhattan. The indulgent use of quince jam and the delicious edible garnish make this a fancy showstopper of a drink that will impress the most discerning guests.

Pritesh Mody, World of Zing

INGREDIENTS

- 1¾ ounces Burnt Faith brandy
- 1 teaspoon quince jam
- ⅓ ounce Cocchi Vermouth di Torino
- ⅓ ounce Cocchi Vermouth di Torino Extra Dry
- 2 dashes Angostura® aromatic bitters

GARNISH

* Pecorino Toscano slice

GLASS

* Coupe, chilled

METHOD

1. Stir the brandy and quince jam together in a mixing glass until they have combined.
2. Add all the remaining ingredients and some ice and stir until chilled.
3. Fine strain into a chilled coupe.
4. Garnish with a pecorino Toscano slice.

Pecorino Toscano is a deliciously hard, salty, tangy cheese made from sheep's milk. An aged Spanish manchego is also made from sheep's milk and can be a suitable substitute.

AMARANTH

Elevated, nutty, herbal

This is a twist on a Brandy Alexander, a dessert cocktail that was popular in the early 20th century. This brandy classic is taken to new heights with two spirits, cognac and rum, as well as sherry, bitters, and amaranth—a gluten-free grain with a nutty, herbal, slightly peppered taste.

Recipe inspired by Krystian Kropaczewski, Artesian Bar, London, 2023

INGREDIENTS

- 1 ounce cognac
- ½ ounce Angostura 1824 rum
- ⅓ ounce oloroso sherry
- ⅔ ounce amaranth orgeat (see below)
- 2 dashes Angostura® aromatic bitters
- 2 drops saline solution
- ⅔ ounce heavy cream

GARNISH

* Amaranth grain chaff and an edible flower

GLASS

* Coupe

METHOD

1. Add cognac, rum, sherry, and amaranth orgeat to a mixing glass with ice.
2. Add the bitters and saline solution.
3. Stir for 15 seconds and strain into a coupe.
4. Float the heavy cream over the top.

To make amaranth orgeat, blend 3½ ounces of amaranth grain into a fine flour and toast in a pan over a medium heat for 10 minutes until dark brown, stirring constantly to avoid burning. Once cool, combine one part toasted flour with six parts water and strain the mixture through a cheesecloth. Add roughly ½ cup of sugar and stir over low heat to make a syrup. Once cool, add 2 drops of orange blossom water. Store in a glass bottle in the refrigerator for up to a month.

Angostura bitters are a kitchen staple and not just for cocktails. In Trinidad and Tobago, bitters are frequently used in food as well as drinks—from a few dashes in your morning coffee and fruit juice to rum punches and, of course, cocktails. Look closely at a bottle of bitters, and you'll see suggestions for how to use it to impart exquisite flavor to a wide range of foods, from soups, salads, and meat dishes to desserts.

Bitters can be enjoyed all the way through dinner and beyond. But if you're unsure of how to get started, here are some simple pairing suggestions. Like in cocktails, bitters help bind flavors together. Orange bitters add a citrusy depth of flavor to dishes, while rich and nutty cocoa bitters are perfect for desserts. You'll often need more generous servings of bitters in food, regularly opting for spoonfuls versus dashes.

PART 2. FOOD

★

SAVORY

In the same way that bitters add depth of flavor to iconic cocktails such as the Old-Fashioned, they can also be used to enhance your favorite savory dishes. It's the perfect secret ingredient—just a few dashes can elevate your dishes and delight your guests.

SUMPTUOUS SOUPS

In the Caribbean, it's not unusual to add a teaspoon of Angostura® aromatic bitters to broth. Like with an Old-Fashioned, you may not initially notice the bitters, but you'll certainly notice their absence once you get used to them.

ADDING DEPTH TO SAUCES

Even your standard ketchup can be enhanced with a few dashes of bitters. For a winning finishing touch to a classic barbecue sauce, try adding a few dashes of Angostura® cocoa bitters for an incredibly rich depth of flavor.

SENSATIONAL SALADS

There are lots of ways to use bitters in salad dressings. Try adding them to enrich mayonnaise dressings with some fresh lemon juice and grated Parmesan cheese. Adding orange bitters to an olive oil–based dressing adds a zesty fragrance, while cocoa bitters can stand up well to the deeper flavors of balsamic-based dressings.

FRAGRANT RICE

To add a zesty fragrance to coconut rice, cook 10½ ounces of white rice as per package instructions. Separately combine 1 tablespoon of butter, 1 tablespoon of orange bitters, 1 teaspoon of salt, ¼ teaspoon of nutmeg, and a pinch of cayenne pepper. Stir this mixture into the cooked rice and then fold in 3½ ounces of shredded coconut, 1¼ ounces of chopped spring onions, and the zest of 1 orange.

MAKE SEAFOOD SING

Orange bitters add a zesty, bright lift to fish dishes, and 1 tablespoon of bitters works wonderfully in a lemon garlic marinade for shrimp. All you need to do is combine 2½ ounces of olive oil with the zest of 1 lemon, 1½ tablespoons of chopped fresh parsley, a couple of crushed cloves of garlic, 1 teaspoon of salt, and as much or as little chili pepper as you can handle. At the end, add 1 tablespoon of bitters to bind all those flavors together.

UP YOUR CHILI GAME

To elevate your chili con carne, all it takes is 2 tablespoons of bitters. Cook the onions and garlic, brown the meat, and then add the bitters along with the other chili ingredients. Bring to a boil, cover, and simmer for 20 minutes. Remove the lid and simmer for a final 30 minutes.

MARINATING MEATS

Meat dishes in the Caribbean are always so succulent and flavorful. The secret is often brining meat in a mixture of water, salt, sugar, and spices before cooking. This serves to clean, moisturize, and tenderize the meat and keep it fresh and juicy once cooked. After brining, it's then marinated. Caribbean cooking is big on flavor, and the secret ingredient in a marinade is often a few good dashes of bitters.

GLAZING HAM

For a sensational flavor twist on an easy yet impressive main dish, brush ham with a bitter honey glaze. Stir together 8 tablespoons of honey, 2 tablespoons of fresh lemon juice, and 1 teaspoon of bitters, then glaze away!

SWEET

In the book celebrating our centenary in 1924, there were a number of suggestions as to how to use bitters in desserts. While some of the recipes, such as blancmanges and cabinet puddings, have fallen out of fashion, others such as fruit salads, sponge cakes, and ice cream are still perennial favorites and have stood the test of time—like bitters themselves.

FRUIT SALAD

Angostura® aromatic bitters work well in fruit juices, and the same can be said for fruit salads. A few dashes add a subtle and delicate distinction that brings the natural fruit flavors to the fore.

APPLE CRUMBLE

Bitters work well in apple-based cocktails, such as the Stone Fence (page 32), so it stands to reason that they add the same richness and depth to the crispy topping of this traditional autumnal dessert. Add bitters to the butter, then combine with the flour, oats, and sugar for an exceedingly good crumble topping.

TRIFLE

Add a few dashes of bitters to the fruit gelatin section of a trifle before setting and watch it boost the flavors with very little added effort.

ADDING RICHNESS TO CHOCOLATE TREATS

Both cocoa and orange bitters enliven chocolate desserts, either with a nutty richness or a citrus lift.

PASTRIES

Orange bitters have a magnificent yet delicate scent that livens up pastries. Add 1 teaspoon to your raw pastry dough and enjoy the enhanced aromas.

A CLASSIC SPONGE MADE BETTER

Bitters appear in a classic sponge cake in our centenary book from 1924: "Beat the yolks of 4 eggs until thick and creamy, add ⅔ cup of sugar, a little at a time, beating with an egg beater, add 3 teaspoons Angostura aromatic bitters, then the whites of the eggs, beaten until still. When the whites are partly mixed with the yolks and sugar, add ⅔ cup of sifted flour mixed with 1 teaspoon salt. Bake for 1 hour."

ICE CREAM TOPPING

Drizzle aromatic or orange bitters on ice cream. Or go one step further and make a bitters-rich chocolate sauce to drizzle over your ice cream. You can do this by combining 2 ounces of milk, 3½ ounces of cocoa powder, 2 teaspoons of Angostura® aromatic bitters, and 2 teaspoons of brandy.

PUMPKIN PIE

Add 2 teaspoons of orange bitters at the same time as the pumpkin to your pumpkin pie and just wait for your guests to ask what your secret ingredient is. It's a game changer.

BEIGNETS

Add a generous quantity of cocoa bitters to your raw beignet dough and, once fried, you can finish these fluffy choux pastry balls with a dusting of powdered sugar and more dashes of cocoa bitters for good measure.

ACKNOWLEDGMENTS

This is not the first time Angostura has created a cocktail book. *Dr. Siegert's Angostura Bitters*, published in 1906, includes "recipes for mixing fancy drinks," many of which are today's classic cocktails. In 1924, Angostura published the *Centenary Gift Book of Cocktail and Other Recipes* to celebrate the brand's 100th anniversary. As a result, our latest cocktail book feels a little like picking up the baton and continuing the work of showcasing some of the incredible drinks made possible with Angostura.

We would like to thank the employees of Angostura for their unwavering dedication and continuous support. Their expertise has propelled the company to new heights, driving innovation and setting industry standards. With a deep understanding of the market and a commitment to excellence, they have successfully navigated challenges and seized opportunities, ensuring the company's sustained growth and success.

It is crucial to also thank the countless bartenders around the world who chose to develop recipes with Angostura bitters over the past 200 years, and to the many who took the time to document these recipes, which have been passed down over the past two centuries for generations to come. We would like to pay our respects to the late Gérard A. Besson, a historian who ensured that so much of Angostura's rich history and fabled stories have been protected and documented for posterity.

A special thank-you to all the bartenders who have entered the Angostura Global Cocktail Challenges for the past 10 years and those using Angostura bitters on menus today, who are helping to create and inspire more modern classic cocktails.

This cocktail book celebrates a historic 200 years of Angostura bitters. Here's to another 200!

HOUSE OF
CELEBRATING
1824
2024
200 YEARS
ANGOSTURA

INDEX

Note: Page numbers in **bold** *refer to recipe illustrations.*

4-Way Citrus Shrub 136, **137**

absinthe
  Butterfly Swizzle 70, **71**
  Tuxedo 42, **43**
absinthe (La Fée NV Absinthe Verte), Mandarin Sazerac 112, **113**
agave nectar 114, 166
Alaska 44, **45**
alcohol-free/low-alcohol cocktails 123–44
allspice syrup 128, **129**
Amaranth 192, **193**
amaranth orgeat, homemade, Amaranth 192, **193**
Amaretti Sour 140, **141**
amaro, Black Manhattan 180, **181**
amaro di Angostura®
  Amaro Bank Burst 188, **189**
  Butterfly Swizzle 70, **71**
Angostura® 5-year-old rum
  Doctor's Orders 186, **187**
  Five Island Fizz 64, **65**
  Mai Tai 60, **61**
  The Charmer 162, **163**
Angostura® 7-year-old rum
  Butterfly Swizzle 70, **71**
  Queen's Park Swizzle 54, **55**
Angostura® 200-year anniversary limited edition bitters 19
  Classique 20, **21**
  VIP Paloma 22, **23**
Angostura® 1824 rum
  Amaranth 192, **193**
  Classique 20, **21**
  Old Flame 118, **119**
  Rum Manhattan 46, **47**
Angostura® 1919 rum
  Amaro Bank Burst 188, **189**
  Daiquiri 58, **59**
  Old Cuban 62, **63**
Angostura® aromatic bitters 18, 198–9
  4-Way Citrus Shrub 136, **137**
  Amaranth 192, **193**
  Amaretti Sour 140, **141**
  Amaro Bank Burst 188, **189**
  Bamboo 154, **155**
  Black Manhattan 180, **181**
  Boothby Cocktail 156, **157**
  Butterfly Swizzle 70, **71**
  Champagne Cocktail 34, **35**
  Champs-Élysées 178, **179**
  Cheese Board Manhattan 190, **191**
  Chet Baker 110, **111**
  Clover Club 82, **83**
  Cuban Chawari 166, **167**
  Daiquiri 58, **59**
  Doctor Limebender 68, **69**
  Fitzgerald 108, **109**
  Five Island Fizz 64, **65**
  Green Mind Collins 132, **133**
  Japanese Cocktail 36, **37**
  Johann Goes to Mexico 96, **97**
  Juliet and Romeo 94, **95**
  Lemon, Lime, and Bitters 126, **127**
  Mai Tai 60, **61**
  Mandarin Sazerac 112, **113**
  Manhattan 38, **39**
  Martinez 104, **105**
  Media Combinación 160, **161**
  Mr. Brown 182, **183**
  New York Sour 80, **81**
  No-groni 142, **143**
  Oaxacan Old-Fashioned 114, **115**
  Obelix 144, **145**
  Old Cuban 62, **63**
  Old-Fashioned 30, **31**
  Old Flame 118, **119**
  Pegu Club 88, **89**
  Pink Gin 150, **151**
  Pisco Sour 84, **85**
  Queen's Park Swizzle 54, **55**
  Rosita 106, **107**
  Rum Manhattan 46, **47**
  Rye Tai 66, **67**
  Singapore Sling 56, **57**
  Sippin' on Gin and Juice 72, **73**
  Sober Summer Cup 134, **135**
  Star 40, **41**
  Stone Fence 32, **33**
  The Bennett 48, **49**
  The Charmer 162, **163**
  The Line Cocktail 86, **87**
  The Scarlet Ibis 116, **117**
  Trinidad Sour 78, **79**
  Trinity 158, **159**
Angostura® Chill 126
Angostura® cocoa bitters 7, 18–19, 194, 196, 198–9
  Cacao Negroni 168, **169**

Café Trinidad 184, **185**
Espresso Martini 174, **175**
Nut Ah Colada 138, **139**
Twin Cities 120, **121**
Angostura® orange bitters 7, 13, 18, 194, 196–9
Alaska 44, **45**
Amaro Bank Burst 188, **189**
Bamboo 154, **155**
Bijou 176, **177**
Black Manhattan 180, **181**
Boothby Cocktail 156, **157**
Bourbon Highball 164, **165**
Butterfly Swizzle 70, **71**
Café Trinidad 184, **185**
Doctor's Orders 186, **187**
London Calling 92, **93**
Martini 101, 102, **103**
Mr. Brown 182, **183**
No-groni 142, **143**
Old Flame 118, **119**
Pegu Club 88, **89**
Rosita 106, **107**
Tuxedo 42, **43**
Viejísimo Adonis 152, **153**
Winter 75 128, **129**
Angostura® reserva white rum, Mai Tai 60, **61**
aperitif wine (Lillet Blanc), Classique 20, **21**
aperitifs 147–68
apple brandy, Star 40, **41**
apple crumble 198
apple juice
Green Mind Collins 132, **133**
Stone Fence 32, **33**
apricot liqueur, Twin Cities 120, **121**
aquafaba 140

Bamboo 154, **155**
banana liqueur, Butterfly Swizzle 70, **71**
barspoons 15
basil leaves 186, **187**
bay leaf foam 162, **163**
beignets 199
Bénédictine liqueur
Singapore Sling 56, **57**
The Charmer 162, **163**
The Line Cocktail 86, **87**
Bennett, The 48, **49**
Bijou 176, **177**
Black Manhattan 180, **181**
Bolognese, Valentino 77
Boon, Ngiam Tong 56
Boothby, William T. 156
Boothby Cocktail 156, **157**
botanicals 8, 10, 18–19
Bourbon Highball 164, **165**
Bradsell, Dick 173
brandy
ice cream toppings 199
Stone Fence 32, **33**
see also apple brandy
brandy (Burnt Faith), Cheese Board Manhattan 190, **191**
Butterfly Swizzle 70, **71**

Cacao Negroni 168, **169**
Café Trinidad 184, **185**
cakes 199
Campari, Rosita 106, **107**
Campari (cacao-infused), Cacao Negroni 168, **169**
celery syrup 132, **133**
Champagne
Boothby Cocktail 156, **157**
Champagne Cocktail 7, 34, **35**
Classique 20, **21**
Old Cuban 62, **63**
Champs-Élysées 178, **179**
Chardonnay vinegar 136
Charmer, The 162, **163**
Chartreuse (green)
Bijou 176, **177**
Champs-Élysées 178, **179**
Chartreuse (yellow)
Alaska 44, **45**
The Scarlet Ibis 116, **117**
Cheese Board Manhattan 190, **191**
cherry liqueur (Heering), Singapore Sling 56, **57**
cherry oysters, drunk 116, **117**
Chet Baker 110, **111**
chili 197
chili-infused Pedro Ximénez sherry, Old Flame 118, **119**
chocolate 198
Classique 20, **21**
Clover Club 82, **83**
club soda
4-Way Citrus Shrub 136, **137**
Bourbon Highball 164, **165**
Fruity Buck 130, **131**
Green Mind Collins 132, **133**

club soda (*continued*)
Singapore Sling 56, **57**
see also grapefruit soda; lemon-lime soda; pink soda
coconut cream 138, **139**
coconut milk 186, **187**
coconut rice 197
coconut water 188, **189**
coffee liqueur
Espresso Martini 174, **175**
Mr. Brown 182, **183**
cognac
Amaranth 192, **193**
Champagne Cocktail 34, **35**
Champs-Élysées 178, **179**
Japanese Cocktail 36, **37**
cognac (Pierre Ferrand 1840), Twin Cities 120, **121**
cola, Sober Summer Cup 134, **135**
Craddock, Harry 7, 13
cream
Amaranth 192, **193**
Café Trinidad 184, **185**
crumble, apple 198
Cuban Chawari 166, **167**
cucumber slices
Juliet and Romeo 94, **95**
Sober Summer Cup 134, **135**
Cunningham, Marv 188

Daiquiri 58, **59**
DeGroff, Dale 108
demerara syrup 54, 96, 184
digestifs 171–92
Doctor Limebender 68, **69**
Doctor's Orders 186, **187**
Dogg, Snoop 51, 72
Dorman, Meaghan 48

egg white
Amaretti Sour 140, **141**
bay leaf foam 162, **163**
Clover Club 82, **83**
New York Sour 80, **81**
Pisco Sour 84, **85**
replacements 140
Trinidad Sour 78
espresso
Café Trinidad 184, **185**
Espresso Martini 174, **175**

fig leaf–infused Keeper's Heart Irish + American Whiskey, Twin Cities 120, **121**
Fitzgerald 108, **109**
Five Island Fizz 64, **65**
fruit salad 198

Giffard Abricot du Roussillon apricot liqueur, Twin Cities 120, **121**
Giffard Aperitif Syrup, No-groni 142, **143**
gin 13
Alaska 44, **45**
Bijou 176, **177**
Fitzgerald 108, **109**
Juliet and Romeo 94, **95**
London Calling 92, **93**
Martinez 104, **105**
Martini 102, **103**
Pegu Club 88, **89**
Pink Gin 6, 150, **151**
Singapore Sling 56, **57**
The Bennett 48, **49**
Trinity 158, **159**
Tuxedo 42, **43**
gin (alcohol-free), No-groni 142, **143**
gin (Bayab rose water), Cacao Negroni 168, **169**
gin (dry), The Line Cocktail 86, **87**
gin (hibiscus-and-rosehip-infused), Sippin' on Gin and Juice 72, **73**
gin (London dry)
Clover Club 82, **83**
Media Combinación 160, **161**
ginger ale, Sober Summer Cup 134, **135**
ginger beer (Barritt's), Five Island Fizz 64, **65**
ginger syrup, homemade, Fruity Buck 130, **131**
glasses 17
glazes 197
González, Giuseppe 77, 78
grapefruit soda, VIP Paloma 22, **23**
Green Mind Collins 132, **133**
guava syrup, homemade, Doctor Limebender 68, **69**

habanero-infused tequila, Doctor Limebender 68, **69**
ham, glazes 197
Hemingway, Ernest 58
highballs 13
honey, The Charmer 162, **163**
honey syrup, homemade, Chet Baker 110, **111**

ice cream toppings 199

Japanese Cocktail 36, **37**
jiggers 14
Johann Goes to Mexico 96, **97**
Johnson, Harry 176
Jones, Daniyel 162
Juliet and Romeo 94, **95**

kit 14–15

lemon juice
Amaretti Sour 140, **141**
Champs-Élysées 178, **179**
Clover Club 82, **83**
Fitzgerald 108, **109**
Fruity Buck 130, **131**
Green Mind Collins 132, **133**
Johann Goes to Mexico 96, **97**
London Calling 92, **93**

New York Sour 80, **81**
Rye Tai 66, **67**
Sober Summer Cup 134, **135**
Trinidad Sour 78, **79**
Winter 75 128, **129**
lemon-lime soda
Lemon, Lime, and Bitters 126, **127**
Sober Summer Cup 134, **135**
lemongrass syrup (spicy), homemade, Amaro Bank Burst 188, **189**
lime juice
Butterfly Swizzle 70, **71**
Daiquiri 58, **59**
Doctor Limebender 68, **69**
Doctor's Orders 186, **187**
Five Island Fizz 64, **65**
Juliet and Romeo 94, **95**
Lemon, Lime, and Bitters 126, **127**
Mai Tai 60, **61**
Old Cuban 62, **63**
Pegu Club 88, **89**
Pisco Sour 84, **85**
Queen's Park Swizzle 54, **55**
Singapore Sling 56, **57**
The Bennett 48, **49**
The Charmer 162, **163**
lime syrup, Obelix 144, **145**
Line Cocktail, The 86, **87**
London Calling 92, **93**
Lyre Apéritif Rosso, No-groni 142, **143**
Lyre's Amaretti, Amaretti Sour 140, **141**

Madeira, The Scarlet Ibis 116, **117**
Mai Tai 60, **61**
mandarin juice, Doctor's Orders 186, **187**
Mandarine Napoléon liqueur, Mandarin Sazerac 112, **113**
Manhattan 7, 38, **39**
see also Cheese Board Manhattan; Star
maple syrup 130
maraschino cherry liqueur
frozen Daiquiri 58
Martinez 104, **105**
Tuxedo 42, **43**
maraschino cherries (Luxardo), liqueur from, Five Island Fizz 64, **65**
Margarita 90, **91**
marinades 197
Martinez 104, **105**
Martini 13, 14, 100–2, **103**
see also Alaska; Espresso Martini; Tuxedo
McKone, Joseph F. 152
meats 197
medals 11
Media Combinación 160, **161**
mezcal, Oaxacan Old-Fashioned 114, **115**
mezcal (Vida), Johann Goes to Mexico 96, **97**
milk, Nut Ah Colada 138, **139**
mint leaves
Juliet and Romeo 94, **95**
Old Cuban 62, **63**
Queen's Park Swizzle 54, **55**
Sober Summer Cup 134, **135**
mixology 24
Morris, Victor Vaughen 84
Mr. Brown 182, **183**
muddlers 15
Muyu Jasmine Verte liqueur, Cuban Chawari 166, **167**

Negroni, *see* Cacao Negroni
Negroni, Count Camillo 168
New York Sour 80, **81**
No-groni 142, **143**
Nut Ah Colada 138, **139**

Oaxacan Old-Fashioned 114, **115**
Obelix 144, **145**
Old Cuban 62, **63**
Old-Fashioned 7, 28–30, **31**
see also Oaxacan Old-Fashioned
Old Flame 118, **119**
Onojiro-Noriyuki, Tateishi 36
orange curaçao
Mai Tai 60, **61**
Media Combinación 160, **161**
Pegu Club 88, **89**
orange juice, Sober Summer Cup 134, **135**
orgeat syrup
Japanese Cocktail 36, **37**
Mai Tai 60, **61**
Rye Tai 66, **67**
Sippin' on Gin and Juice 72, **73**
Trinidad Sour 78, **79**

pastries 199
peanut butter, Nut Ah Colada 138, **139**
Pegu Club 88, **89**
Petraske, Sasha 130
pies, pumpkin 199
pineapple juice
Fruity Buck 130, **131**
Nut Ah Colada 138, **139**
Obelix 144, **145**
Rye Tai 66, **67**
Singapore Sling 56, **57**
Sippin' on Gin and Juice 72, **73**
Pink Gin 6, 148–50, **151**
pink soda (Schweppes Russchian), Obelix 144, **145**
Pisco Sour 84, **85**
Prohibition 29, 32, 46, 58
Prosecco, VIP Paloma 22, **23**
Proulx, Theodore 29
pumpkin pie 199

Quararibea turbinata tree 15, 53
Queen's Park Swizzle 52–4, **55**
quince jam, Cheese Board Manhattan 190, **191**

Raffles Bar 56
raspberry syrup
Clover Club 82, **83**
Obelix 144, **145**
red wine, New York Sour 80, **81**
Regan, Gary "Gaz" 106
Reiner, Julie 82
rice, coconut 197
Rob Roy 38
rose water, Juliet and Romeo 94, **95**
Rosita 106, **107**
royal warrants 6, 11
rum
Rum Manhattan 46, **47**
see also Angostura® 5-year-old rum; Angostura® 7-year-old rum; Angostura® 1824 rum; Angostura® 1919 rum; Angostura® reserva white rum
rum (aged)
Chet Baker 110, **111**
Stone Fence 32, **33**
rum (Caribbean spiced), Cuban Chawari 166, **167**
rum (golden), Old Cuban 62, **63**
Rye Tai 66, **67**

salad dressings 196
saline solution 192
salt 90, 94, 116
sauces 196
Saunders, Audrey 62
savory dishes 196–7
Scarlet Ibis, The 116, **117**
seafood 197
shakers 14
sherry (amontillado), Tuxedo 42, **43**
sherry (chili-infused Pedro Ximénez), Old Flame 118, **119**
sherry (fino)
Bamboo 154, **155**
London Calling 92, **93**
Tuxedo 42, **43**
sherry (Lustau VORS amontillado), Viejísimo Adonis 152, **153**
sherry (Lustau East India Solera cream sherry), Viejísimo Adonis 152, **153**
sherry (oloroso)
Amaranth 192, **193**
Cuban Chawari 166, **167**
sherry vinegar 162
Shrub, 4-Way Citrus 136, **137**
Siegert, Dr. Johann 6, 11, 96
simple syrup
Amaretti Sour 140, **141**
Butterfly Swizzle 70, **71**
Champs-Élysées 178, **179**
Clover Club 82, **83**
Daiquiri 58, **59**
Espresso Martini 174, **175**
Fitzgerald 108, **109**
Juliet and Romeo 94, **95**
London Calling 92, **93**
Mandarin Sazerac 112, **113**
New York Sour 80, **81**
Old Cuban 62, **63**
Old-Fashioned 30, **31**
Pisco Sour 84, **85**
Singapore Sling 13, 56, **57**
Sippin' on Gin and Juice 72, **73**
slings 13
see also Singapore Sling
Sober Summer Cup 134, **135**
soda. *See* grapefruit soda; lemon-lime soda; pink soda
soups 196
sours 13
see also Amaretti Sour; New York Sour; Pisco Sour; Trinidad Sour
sparkling wine (alcohol-free), Winter 75 128, **129**
sponge 199
Star 40, **41**
Stone Fence 32, **33**
strainers 15
strawberries, Sober Summer Cup 134, **135**
strawberry cordial, homemade, Doctor's Orders 186, **187**
styles of drink 12–13
sugar cubes 34, **35**
sweet dishes 198–9
swizzle sticks 13, 15, 53–4
swizzlestick tree 15, 53
swizzles 13
Butterfly Swizzle 70, **71**
Queen's Park Swizzle 52–4, **55**

tamarind pulp, Amaro Bank Burst 188, **189**
tea (Taiwanese black), Cuban Chawari 166, **167**
tequila (agave blanco), Margarita 90, **91**
tequila (agave reposado), VIP Paloma 22, **23**
tequila (reposado)
Oaxacan Old-Fashioned 114, **115**
Rosita 106, **107**
tequila (Tapatio 110 proof), Doctor Mindbender 68, **69**
tequila (Tapatio blanco), Doctor Mindbender 68, **69**
Thomas, "Professor" Jerry 32, 36, 152
Trader Vic (Victor Bergeron Jr.) 60
trifle 198
Trinidad Sour 76–8, **79**
Trinidad and Tobago 6–8, 10, 18, 53, 54, 64, 116, 118, 126, 184, 188, 194
Trinity 158, **159**
triple sec
Margarita 90, **91**
Sippin' on Gin and Juice 72, **73**
Tuxedo 42, **43**
Twin Cities 120, **121**

vanilla syrup, homemade, Mr. Brown 182, **183**
Velvet Falernum, Five Island Fizz 64, **65**
verjus blanc, Twin Cities 120, **121**
vermouth, storage 158

vermouth (Cocchi di Torino Extra Dry), Cheese Board Manhattan 190, **191**
vermouth (Cocchi Vermouth di Torino)
Cheese Board Manhattan 190, **191**
Twin Cities 120, **121**
vermouth (dry)
Bamboo 154, **155**
Martini 102, **103**
Rosita 106, **107**
vermouth (French), martinis 13
vermouth (French dry)
Clover Club 82, **83**
Trinity 158, **159**
vermouth (Italian sweet), Trinity 158, **159**
vermouth (Lustau red vermouth), Viejísimo Adonis 152, **153**
vermouth (rose), Cacao Negroni 168, **169**
vermouth (Spanish red), Media Combinación 160, **161**
vermouth (sweet)
Bijou 176, **177**
Boothby Cocktail 156, **157**
Chet Baker 110, **111**
Manhattan 38, **39**
Martinez 104, **105**
Rosita 106, **107**
Rum Manhattan 46, **47**
Star 40, **41**
The Line Cocktail 86, **87**
Vidal, Camille 128
Viejísimo Adonis 152, **153**
VIP Paloma 22, **23**
vodka, Espresso Martini 174, **175**

whiskey (bourbon)
Boothby Cocktail 156, **157**
Bourbon Highball 164, **165**
Fitzgerald 108, **109**
Mr. Brown 182, **183**
New York Sour 80, **81**
Old-Fashioned 30, **31**
Stone Fence 32, **33**
whiskey (fig leaf-infused Keeper's Heart Irish + American), Twin Cities 120, **121**
whiskey (Maker's Mark), Mandarin Sazerac 112, **113**
whiskey (rye)
Black Manhattan 180, **181**
Boothby Cocktail 156, **157**
Manhattan 38, **39**
Old-Fashioned 30, **31**
Rye Tai 66, **67**
Stone Fence 32, **33**
Trinidad Sour 78, **79**
whisky (Bunnahabhain 12 year old), The Scarlet Ibis 116, **117**
whisky (Scotch), Rob Roy 38
Winter 75 128, **129**

Originally published in 2024 in Great Britain by Ebury Press, an imprint of Ebury Publishing, as *Classic Cocktails and Fancy Drinks with Angostura® Bitters.*

Text © Ebury Press 2024
Photography © Ebury Press 2024

All rights reserved
Printed in Slovenia
First American Edition 2025

For information about permission to reproduce selections from this book, write to Permissions, Countryman Press, 500 Fifth Avenue, New York, NY 10110

For information about special discounts for bulk purchases, please contact W. W. Norton Special Sales at specialsales@wwnorton.com or 800-233-4830

Design: Sandra Zellmer with Kasia Roy
Photography: Haarala Hamilton
Drinks Stylist: Tom Woodward
Prop Stylist: Hannah Wilkinson
Angostura® Bitters Consultant: Vitra Deonarine
Angostura® Bitters Coordinator: Janeen Frection
Writer: Sarah Belizaire
Manufacturing by DZS Grafik

Countryman Press
www.countrymanpress.com

An imprint of W. W. Norton & Company, Inc.
500 Fifth Avenue, New York, NY 10110
www.wwnorton.com

978-1-68268-990-5

1 2 3 4 5 6 7 8 9 0